McKay has courageously decided to say "No to Cussing" like saying "No to Drugs" or "No to Smoking." He has prevailed. McKay has built a growing army of supporters and is cleaning up communications worldwide. I am cheering him on as you will when you read his inspired book.

—Mark Victor Hansen
Co-creator, #1 New York Times best-selling series *Chicken Soup for the Soul*®
Co-author, *Cracking the Millionaire Code* and *The One Minute Millionaire*

McKay's story is one of courage. I met McKay in California and his story of the No Cussing Club is an inspiration to us all to never give up and to stand up for what you believe in.

—Rudy Ruettiger, past football player for Notre Dame
From the movie *Rudy*

This is a fantastic book, written by a young man who possesses a lot of courage.... This is an interesting read, well written in a simple and easy-to-follow style, and is loaded with anecdotes and statistics. As McKay shares a lot of stories about kids, this book is acceptable for children old enough to read it and in fact we would encourage kids to read it. We gladly award this book our Dove "Family-Approved" Seal. Way to go McKay! Keep up the good work.

—Erwin L. Carpenter, The Dove Foundation

The
No
Cussing
Club™

The
No
Cussing
Club™

How I Fought Against Peer Pressure and How You Can Too

McKay Hatch

Dawson Publishing
www.NoCussing.com

ISBN: 9780945713081

Library of Congress Control Number: 2008904763

Project management by Brent Hatch, Cary Inouye, Cecily Markland
Editing by Cecily Markland, Inglestone Publishing, www.InglestonePublishing.com
Proofreading by Chelsea Combs
Illustrations by Todd White, www.TWhiteIllustration.com
Photography by Roclord Studios, http://www.Roclord.com

Publishing services provided by Jorlan Publishing:
Book cover design by Becky Fawson
Book design and layout by Marny K. Parkin
www.JorlanPublishing.com

Printed in the United States
10 9 8 7 6 5 4 3 2 1

Dawson Publishing, Inc.
P.O. Box 65
South Pasadena, CA 91031

Contents

Acknowledgments

I never could have started the No Cussing Club and this book never would have happened without a lot of help from a lot of people. I want especially to thank my parents, Brent and Phelecia Hatch, and my brothers and sisters. They have been awesome in so many ways. Thanks, too, to all of my cousins and friends from school and church, who supported me from Day 1. I also would like to say thanks to Bill Glazier, the editor of my local paper, for believing in my story and running it first. Also, my middle school principal, Mercedes Metz, for giving me great advice. I appreciate Mayor Cacciotti and the South Pasadena City Council for giving our club the first-ever city proclamation for a Cuss Free Week and Arroyo Vista Elementary School, South Pasadena Middle School, and South Pasadena High School for supporting our cause and putting the Cuss Free Week on their marquees.

A big thank you goes to my uncle Cary Inouye for helping me with the songs, videos, and too many other things to list; to my other uncle Ethan Willis for his advice and direction; to Laurie Liss for all of her expert feedback on my manuscript; and to Cecily Markland for putting up with me and my dad and for her excellent suggestions and changes to the manuscript.

Last, I appreciate so much all the members of the No Cussing Club from all over the world. This would not be a club without you!

Thank you,
McKay Hatch,
Founder of the No Cussing Club

Introducing:
The No Cussing Club

J ust a few months ago, only a few hundred people had heard
of 14-year-old McKay Hatch. He was known by those on his
soccer team, by people from his church, by his friends at school
and by the other guys in his Scout troop.

That was before McKay stood up to his friends and said
two simple words: "Don't cuss."

Today, because of that one statement, tens of thousands of
people—perhaps even hundreds of thousands—have heard of
McKay. He has an impressive list of fans—from Los Angeles
Sheriff Joe Baca; to U.S. Congressman from California, Adam
Schiff; to American Idol host, Ryan Seacrest, and other celeb-
rities and government and community leaders.

McKay has been on television all over the world, including on CNN, the Dr. Phil Show and MSNBC, as well as many,
many other television and radio programs. He has presented
workshops in several states and has been selected for awards,
like the Well Done Award from The Kingdom Assignment™
Foundation and a "family-approved" recognition from The

Dove Foundation. He also has been honored by the Parents Television Council.

Hundreds of thousands of e-mails

In the past two years, McKay has received hundreds of thousands of e-mails. Think about it. Hundreds of thousands of e-mails. That means every day for the past two years he has gotten a few hundred, and some days thousands of e-mails flood his inbox. While most of the e-mails have been positive, many have come laced with profanities and put downs. He's been attacked verbally. He's had death threats against him. He's had his Web site hacked into and has been the subject of countless blog entries, some extremely positive, many disturbingly negative.

All because of that one simple message—two words, really—that McKay spoke to his friends in middle school back in 2007.

Now, that simple challenge—"Don't cuss"—has been transformed into what McKay calls The No Cussing Club. The club is a movement among teens—and that has been adopted by hundreds of concerned adults, as well—to support one another and to encourage others to clean up their language and to avoid profanity, dirty jokes and other disrespectful and demeaning language.

McKay and other members of the club believe that by simply cleaning up their language—by moving away from the trash talk, the constant slurs and the strings of cuss words—and, instead, choosing what they call "language that lifts," they can accomplish the group's foundational motto to "Leave People Better Than You Found Them."

More than 20,000 people choose "No Cussing"

More than 20,000 "members" from every state in the union and from more than two dozen other countries, have logged on to the No Cussing Club Web site to join the club by taking the "No Cussing Challenge."

McKay, now 15, says, "I've learned a lot in the past two years. I've learned about freedom of speech and what that really means. I've learned about bullying and about cyberbullying from having it done to me. And, I've learned a lot about language and how it affects people.

"Oh, and something else—I always heard that one person can make a difference and I guess I learned that was true.

"One person can stand up for what they believe in. One person can change themselves and can help others to do the same. That's one reason I want to share my story. I want people to know they can make a difference too. I want people to know they can leave others better than they found them. I want people to see that small choices can make a big difference and many of those choices begin with what we say. I want people to take the challenge, 'Don't cuss,' and see what a difference it can make in their lives. Don't cuss!"

Getting on the Roller Coaster

I never in a million years thought I would ever see myself on TV and see my name flashed up on the television screen while I was being interviewed on MSNBC. But, that's just what happened and that's just one of hundreds of things that has surprised me over the past two years.

You know, I've always been a little afraid of roller coasters. I like the speed, but I don't really like the ups and downs and not knowing what kind of dip or bump is going to be around the next curve. It makes me wonder if I really would have gone for the ride I'm on now if I had known just what kind of a roller coaster I was getting onto. I've had almost two years of ups and downs, of times I wanted to get off and of times that were the most thrilling and exciting you can imagine.

It all began in middle school

It all began in 2007, when I was 14. I had grown up in South Pasadena, California, and I am right in the middle of the family, the fourth of my mom and dad's seven kids.

My parents, Brent and Phelecia Hatch, aren't rich, but they have always made sure I have the things I need. They take us to church, want us to work hard, and together we do a lot of things as a family. But, I'm not a nerdy kid or one of those guys who stays home and reads and studies all the time or anything like that. When I was in elementary school, I had a lot of friends and I was always doing something. I was in Boy Scouts and I played on the city soccer leagues. I played a lot of video games, and I liked music and was learning to play different instruments and starting to perform a little.

> **My dad, my teachers, even the mayor of my city and people from all different countries tell me that I've made a difference. Sometimes they even say I've changed the world.**

Really, I was just a regular kid. And, I still am. I'm not really that different from anyone else.

Except, now, my dad, my teachers, even the mayor of my city and people from all different countries tell me that I've made a difference. Sometimes they even say I've changed the world.

I tried to ignore that when some people first said it, but now, in a way, I think they're right. Think about it. If you change the way people see themselves, if you change the way people get along, if you change even a little part of the world, it really can make a huge difference.

I learned that just one 14-year-old, now 15, can do that.

There were times, though, when I wasn't so sure.

This whole thing started when I was going into the 6th grade, my first year of middle school.

We're not in elementary school anymore!

Summer break was over and, like most kids, I wasn't really looking forward to going back to school. But, after a long summer without much to do, I was ready to see all my friends again. Besides, I was excited about being in middle school. We weren't little elementary kids anymore. It was exciting and, at the same time, a little scary—but none of us wanted to admit that. We all just thought it was cool to be in the "big" school where things were new and different.

The first day or two at South Pasadena Middle School, I began to notice that something really was different, something I didn't expect at all. All around me, all the kids—my friends, the kids in the halls, the guys during gym and kids on the bus—were all using bad language. Friends I never heard cuss when we were in 5th grade, now, all of a sudden, in 6th grade, were cussing all the time.

What had happened over the summer? I'm not sure where they learned all these words, maybe they were copying what they heard on TV or in movies or from the music they listened to but they were saying the "A" word, and the "B" word, and on and on, like they almost had a cuss word for every letter of the alphabet. They were saying stuff I had never even heard before. At first, it sort of surprised me, but I didn't say anything. I figured it was no big deal. But, even after a few weeks had gone by, I still couldn't get used to it. That kind of language just didn't sound right coming from them. These were kids I knew, kids I hung out with. They weren't the big troublemakers in the school or anything like that. They were good kids who came from totally cool homes. Their parents were cool. I knew their parents didn't know they were talking like that and wouldn't like it if they did.

Now, I'm not saying that I always did everything my parents taught me or that I never did anything wrong, but cussing was something we had talked about at home and I just didn't want to do it. In Scouting and in elementary school, too, we had learned about respect and about doing our best and I just didn't feel cussing was something I wanted to do.

My friends and I still spent a lot of time together, but their cussing made it hard for me to enjoy being around them. It seemed like they had changed in other ways too. They were, like, all negative— they seemed mad and unhappy all the time.

Talk about Cussing!

Parents and concerned adults—find out more about the cussing that goes on at school and about what your kids hear all the time.

Kids—share with your parents! Let them know what your think about cussing and get their ideas!

Don't get into details about whether it's right or wrong, just get to know each other better and find out what they think!

Parents/adults— Ask your kids:

1. Do you hear a lot of cussing at school?
2. Why do you think kids cuss so much?
3. What do you think kids can do when they hear so much cussing all the time?

Kids— Ask your parents:

1. Did you hear a lot of cussing when you were in school?
2. Why do you think people cuss so much?
3. How do you think cussing affects people?

The thing is, my friends weren't the only ones who were cussing, telling dirty jokes and using bad language all the time. It seemed like everyone was doing it. I don't think most parents have a clue about how much bad language is spoken at school. Some parents may even think there's no cussing problem at all at their kid's school.

That's what my aunt thought. She thought her son's elementary school didn't have that kind of a problem, but, when she told my dad that, he said, "Have you asked your son?" Later, my aunt and uncle talked to their son and they were totally blown away by what they learned. My cousin told them that kids at his elementary school cussed all the time around him. Then my uncle asked him about the "F" word and my cousin said he heard that at his school all the time too. He said, "Dad, you have no idea. It's not only the words, but the things they talk about."

That's how it was at my school too. When that first year of middle school was over, it, was almost nice to come to the end of 6th grade and to spend the summer without hearing cuss words all the time.

But, when we started 7th grade, things seemed to be different again. Now, instead of every cuss word in the book, my friends were using the "F" word all the time. It was like they had to add it to every sentence, like it was the only word they knew.

I remember when we were younger and my brothers and I used to make funny faces and put our fingers in our mouths and stretch them in all different directions. My mom would say, "Don't do that to your face or it will stay that way for the rest of your life." It seemed like that's what my friends had done, like they couldn't do anything else. They were stuck. And, they didn't even know they were doing it. Seriously! It just came out in every sentence and they didn't even realize they were doing it.

By now, it was really starting to bother me. I began to wonder, "Man, is there anyone else at this school who doesn't cuss?"

Odd man out

All of a sudden, I felt like I was odd. I was the strange one. I felt different, like I was the only one who wasn't going along with everyone else in the school.

"Am I going to start cussing too?" I wondered.

I could see why so many kids were doing it. They just want to fit in like everybody else, and they don't know how else to do it. They figure that if they cuss, maybe that's the only way to fit in, to look cool.

But, I really didn't want to do that. Like I said, my mom and dad always taught me good morals, good values; and not cussing was one of them. Besides, what I heard from my friends and others at school didn't make me feel that good and it didn't seem like they were that happy either. Why would I want to do it then?

I didn't want to change and be that way but it seemed like cussing and using bad language was the only way kids were fitting in. I don't even know why it bothered me so much. Most people would think it was just a little thing, maybe, but, for some reason, it was a big thing to me.

What's the Fuss?
Why Not Cuss?

Cussing. It's just a few little words. So, what's the big deal, anyway? My mom and dad and some teachers and other adults had told me it was wrong, but I was beginning to wonder. It didn't seem so wrong to my friends or to any of the other kids at school either.

Back then, I couldn't really put it into words to explain how I felt about cussing. I had to really think and figure it out. I had to ask myself, "So what is this cussing stuff anyway, and is it really so bad?"

I came up with some ideas of why it does bother me, and I'm glad I did, because over the past two years, lots of kids and adults and even news reporters have asked me that question, "What's so bad about cussing?"

Cussing defined

Cussing is sometimes called other things, like "swearing" or "profanity," but you know what I mean by cussing. Many kids know cussing as those words and phrases that get you sent to your room or get your mouth washed out with soap. If you

Cussing by any other name ... It's still cussing!

"Cuss words" or "cussing is sometimes called other things. Have you ever heard cussing or cuss words called any of these things?

- Cursing
- Derogatory language
- Expletives
- Vulgarity
- Swearing
- Profanity
- Epithet
- Four-letter words

- Bad words
- Dirty words
- Strong language
- Irreverent language
- Obscenities
- Potty-mouth words
- "F-bomb," the "s" word, etc.

In cartoons, cussing looks something like this: (%^%#&(*%^$*&!*)*^*%23@!

look in *Webster's College Dictionary* at "cuss word" (or, in some dictionaries, it's listed as one word: cussword), you see this definition: "A profane or obscene word." And, Answers.com says the verb "cussing" means: "To invoke evil or injury upon."

Just going by the definitions (and by your mom's or teacher's reaction) it seems clear that cussing is negative and can be hurtful. Yes, cussing has been around for centuries, but, even still, it seems like it has been considered wrong or negative for all that time. Mark Twain talked about cussing in *The Adventures of Huckleberry Finn*, but he used the word, "cuss," not the cuss word itself. "He ... cussed me for putting on frills and trying to be better than him." In another book, called *Roughing It,* one of Mark Twain's characters even apologized for almost using a cuss word. He writes, "Beg your pardon, friend, for coming so near saying a cuss-word."

These examples show that cussing has long been considered impolite or uncivil and improper. But, today, we hear cuss words used everyday, "F bombs" dropped all over, and dirty jokes told everywhere.

Trash talk

We also hear another kind of language that I feel is part of what I am talking about when I say, "Don't cuss," or especially when I encourage people to use "language that lifts." What I'm talking about is the habit of "put downs," "trash talk," and "dissing" on your friends. "Diss" is a slang word that comes from "disrespect" and, just like cussing and cursing, it is used to insult and to tear people down. Many times you see a group of friends who make a game of this and who think it is funny to throw insults back and forth. While it may seem like a joke at the time, this kind of play is really not fun and, I believe, it can cause a lot of pain that can hurt for many years to come.

Sometimes the dissing goes outside a group of friends and you see kids poking fun or saying rude things about certain cultures, age groups, religions or even people who have handicaps. When language is used in this way, it becomes an awful weapon. I talk about this later in the chapter on bullying, but I want to mention it here because this kind of language is as bad, or worse, than any cuss word and should be on the list of what we are trying to eliminate when we say, "Don't cuss."

Last, as we work to improve our language, we need to remember that certain words are considered sacred to others around us. For me, it bothers me greatly to hear the Lord's name taken in vain. Others may revere, say, Buddah or Allah, and, to them, it is offensive when those names are used irreverently or inappropriately. Doing so is actually a form of cussing.

What's so bad about it, anyway?

So, now you know what I'm talking about when I say, "cussing," but you still may be wondering, "So, what?"

When I was on the *Dr. Phil Show*, he even asked me the same question and he wanted to know why I thought cussing was bad. He asked if I used substitutes, you know, "darn" or "shoot" or other "softer" words in place of cuss words. He said some people might ask, "What's the difference between my combination of letters and the combination of letters that people say are bad words?"

Well, I actually do get a lot of people that ask me that question. If it's not some kid cussing me out, it's some adult getting all philosophical on me. Man, I can't get a break. Seriously, I get a lot of e-mails from adults telling me that what I am doing is wrong because words really have no meaning. They say:

"McKay, you're too young and naïve to understand this but words are just sounds, they don't really mean anything."

"What's in a word, McKay?"

"Who says any word is a bad word?"

Then, I got some other e-mails that used all kinds of big words. (But, then, I guess they don't mean anything, so why don't they just stick with the easy words that take less time to type?) Here's some of the things they said:

"Words are just ambiguous sounds to which there is no true meaning."

"The spectrum of sound waves is an objective phenomenon in which there is no true meaning, only that to which humans have assigned to it in their attempt to manipulate it."

I get stuff like this all the time. I can't tell you how many people have told me, "There's nothing wrong with cussing" and, my favorite, "Words cause no harm, they are meaningless."

Words have meaning

Meaningless? I can't even figure what someone could possibly mean by that. If words are meaningless, how do you ask for, say, a carrot. If the word "carrot" didn't mean one of those orange crunchy things that your mom tells you are good for you, then how in the world would you tell someone to give your rabbit a carrot? But, then, how would they even know you meant the furry animal hopping around the backyard if the word "rabbit" had no meaning?

No, the meaning doesn't come from the letters c-a-r-r-o-t themselves. The meaning comes because people understand and agree that "carrot" means that orange, crunchy object.

I watched the movie *The Miracle Worker* once. It's the story of Helen Keller, who was born blind and deaf. When Helen and her mother first met her teacher, Anne Sullivan, Helen's mother asked the teacher what she would teach Helen first. "Language, I hope," the teacher says. "Language is to the mind more than light to the eye. She has to learn that everything has its name, that words can be her eyes to everything in the world outside her. What is she without words? With them she can think, have ideas, speak, be reached."

That made me think, "What are we without words?" But, what are we if we only use words that are considered bad or ugly, words that are not acceptable to most people? Cuss words—or profanity, or swearing, or cursing, or whatever you want to call it—are words that people generally agree are insulting, rude or disrespectful.

A writer named W. Somerset Maugham believed that words do have meaning and that they have other things too. He said, "Words have weight, sound and appearance; it is only by considering these that you can write a sentence that is good to look at and good to listen to."

Another writer, F. Scott Fitzgerald, said, "You can stroke people with words."

I agree. You can "stroke" people with words, or you can insult them, put them down, and treat them with disrespect—just with the words you use.

Look, I admit that I don't know the history of words and everything, but I do know that in the world I live in, words do have meaning and they do have real effects. Use "potty words" in a school class and you get busted. Use the "F" word in front of most parents and you get royally busted, but not only that, you most likely hurt their feelings as well. Cuss out a player on the other team and you'll get kicked off the field. Swear in a job interview and you probably won't be hired. Or, cuss on the job and you could get fired. (Just ask the men's former basketball coach from Ave Maria University, in southeast Florida, who was fired in September 2008 for "the use of profanity in a scrimmage.") Cuss at your girlfriend and ... well, how would I know, I'm too young to date yet, anyway! Seriously, cuss words—those words some people say don't mean anything—really do mean something. They mean you could find yourself in big trouble, you could ruin friendships, bring on punishment at school and miss out on a good job opportunity or even be fired from a job.

On the other hand, I know there are other words that can do just the opposite. I know what words to say to make my little sister grin. I know that when our team is about to go out on the field, the coach gives us a big speech to pump us up.

I know that when you're feeling down, a friend or your dad can help lift you up by the words they say.

For me, my reasons for not cussing weren't all that philosophical or anything. It was more of a gut feeling, I didn't like the way those words sounded or the way they made me feel. But, as I have thought about this more and tried to learn more, I found something pretty interesting.

Your brain on cussing

I read a thing about the brain and how the brain processes swear words. Language is what they call a "higher" brain function because the processing of language happens in the part of the brain known as the cerebral cortex. But, scientists say swearing is processed in the lower brain, deep inside the brain where emotion and instinct take place. This may sound all scientific and stuff, but what it really is saying is that swearing is more automatic, not something that we have to put a lot of effort into. You've seen that, I'm sure. You've seen someone stub their toe, or burn their dinner, and, almost without thinking, out comes a cuss word.

Swearing and the brain

Language processing takes place in the cerebral cortex, so is

Areas of the Brain that Relate to Language

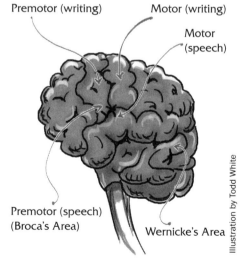

Premotor (writing)

Motor (writing)

Motor (speech)

Premotor (speech) (Broca's Area)

Wernicke's Area

Illustration by Todd White

known as a "higher" brain function. Swearing is like emotion and instinct responses. It is considered a "lower" brain function because it takes place deep inside the brain.

Cuss words are often just a reaction, just something that comes out of our mouths when we don't really care what we're saying. To me, that is saying that swearing is the lazy way out. It doesn't take thinking or any work. Cussing all the time doesn't show that we're trying to better ourselves or anyone around us.

It's even more ridiculous to see how many times a cuss word is used when someone is trying to say something is good, but they can't seem to think of anything better than: "Blankety, blank, that was awesome!" or "Dude, that was blankety, blankety, blank." After a while, it sort of loses its punch. It isn't creative or imaginative and, pretty soon, everything sounds the same. What are you going to say when something really **is** amazing or awesome?

Even children know

Another thing I read said, "Even very young children know which words are naughty, although they don't always know exactly what those words mean."

What is that saying? That some kids cuss even though they don't know what they're saying? I think that's true. I saw a little kid one time who was mad and was just stamping his foot and saying all kinds of words and some things that weren't even words, but he was saying them in a really mean-sounding voice. He didn't know what he was saying, but knew the right tone and just what would get his mom's attention.

The very first newspaper reporter who interviewed me asked me about my reasons for avoiding cussing.

"Clean language is a sign of intelligence," I said at that time.

People who are educated have a better vocabulary, they don't have to use the "F" word in every sentence. They know how to express themselves and they know that language can be a useful tool.

Cussing is seen as language of the lower class

In one article I read, researchers did a study and they found that: "Many people associate the use of swear words with people of lower income and education."

This study didn't say it was only people with lower incomes and less education who swear, or even that they swear more, but it said that people associate swearing with the lower class. What all this says to me is that people who cuss may be educated,

> "The language you use reveals who you are. It can immediately tell people about you. Like the way you dress, for better or worse, people will react to you by the language you use."
> —No Cussing Club member

they may be hard-working and mature—but people who hear them cussing don't see them that way.

One No Cussing Club member put it this way: "The language you use reveals who you are. It can immediately tell people about you. Like the way you dress, for better or worse, people will react to you by the language you use."

And, I like what Christianna Cherf, from Merced, California, wrote in an article in the Merced High School paper back in 2003. Christianna said, "Whether it's fair or not, people are constantly judged on how they talk. The way a person talks can determine their attitude, their background, and even their intelligence. When cussing is wrapped into a person's speech, it presents the person as being angry, dim, or just flat out rude. In our society today, it is obvious to see that the public has, for the most part, adapted to cussing. Not only in schools, but also on TV, in magazines or books, almost anywhere cussing is heard. The real question to ask should be, 'Is cussing actually necessary?'"

I really don't think so!

3
Cussing
Only Gets You
So Far

We could go on for days discussing whether cussing is good or bad and never really settle it. You may think cussing is the worst thing ever, or you may think that there's nothing wrong with it and the rest of the world should just be more accepting of this kind of language. But, that's just the point. Whether it's right or wrong, whether it seems the acceptable thing to do in school or not, the rest of the world—society, or whatever you want to call it, the real world that we will have to function in someday—doesn't consider cussing to be acceptable. There is a difference between what is looked at as "decent and proper" and what is viewed as "bad or indecent language." And, because that's how society views it, cussing has certain consequences, like it or not.

"It's a matter of reality that we attach certain psychological and social meanings to words," says Kelly Crabb, an attorney from Los Angeles, who is also a friend of our family.

He says every culture has certain words that are considered unacceptable.

"I'm one of those people who spent a significant amount of my lifetime learning a foreign language and the language I learned is Japanese. People will say that, typically, Asian languages have less swear words than other languages, but there are a lot of things you can't say in polite company in Japanese. They attach a certain emotional weight to some words, just like we attach a certain emotional weight to certain words in our language. That's just the reality of language."

He told me, "If I said the translation of them, you would probably laugh," and he was right. He said, in polite conversation in Japan, you can't use the word "fool," and you would never call someone a "dirty old man" in Japanese. One of the greatest insults in Japan would be to say the words that, translated into English, mean: "Your child has a twisted belly button."

"I cannot explain it to you, but every language, every culture has words that they apply a certain weight to," he says.

Cussing won't get you that far

In the long run, cussing just won't get you as far as language that is good and appropriate will. It would be like me trying to play soccer but wearing plain old tennis shoes instead of cleats. Tennis shoes would work okay, but cleats help me keep up and compete with others on the field. Clean language could be thought of as your communication cleats—the way to keep up with others and truly succeed in life.

Most of what I've learned about the consequences of cussing has come from the hundreds of e-mails I've received. So many people who have joined the No Cussing Club have written to me to tell me how cussing has affected their lives. They have shared a lot of different stories and all kinds of consequences.

Here are some ways cussing can affect you:

Cussing:

- Can cause people to lose respect for you
- Can hurt others
- Can make problems worse
- Can ruin your opportunities
- Can affect your outlook on yourself and the world.

1. Cussing can cause people to lose respect for you.

Think about it. Why is it important to have people respect you? When people respect you they admire you, they see you have worth. If people don't respect you, they don't want to hire you or do business with you, or spend any time with you at all. One e-mail I received shared an example of how a comedian caused the audience to lose respect for him shows how cussing can affect how other people view you:

You've Got Mail

Dear McKay,

Several years ago, my friends wanted to go to a comedy club in Hollywood. I had never been to a comedy club so I thought it might be fun. The opening acts were actually very funny and filled with acting, dancing, and musical talent. As it got later in the evening however, the acts were less and less funny. It seemed like the language was getting worse too, like they were relying on the bad language for their comedy. It was really just a cover for their poor talent, and not a very good cover at that. Then out on to the stage walks

Skip Stephenson, the guy from that popular '80s TV show, *Real People*. *Real People* was a family show like *America's Funniest Home Videos*. Many times they did stories of people who did heroic things. I thought "finally, something good." I was expecting some Bill Cosby–style humor and was completely floored when he blurted out obscenity after obscenity, crude joke after crude joke. It was not even funny. At that time in my life bad language didn't bother me, but the jokes were just plain NOT FUNNY. The thing is, it completely changed my view of Skip Stephenson. Look, I am no priest and so it may be hypocritical for me to say this, but the fact is, I did lose respect for him. It kind of made me think about my own words. Was that what people thought about me when I cussed?

—Name withheld

2. Cussing can hurt others.

Cussing can insult others and can hurt people's feelings. You can ruin friendships with cussing. The saying, "What goes around, comes around," really applies here. Cuss at someone, and you will probably get cussing in return. So, cussing not only hurts others, but it can hurt you, too. That's what happened with one girl, who says:

You've Got Mail

Dear McKay,

My name is Sarah. I am 16 years old. I used to cuss all the time. I babysit this little girl that is 8 years old and I love her like a sister. I would accidentally cuss in front of her and I knew she didn't like it. One day I cussed in front of her and she started to cry.

I then realized how much it affects some people. From then on, I tried to stop cussing.

—Sarah (Real name withheld)

3. Cussing can make problems worse.

Many people who e-mailed me shared stories about how cussing often made other people mad, made it harder to solve problems and made things worse instead of better. Here's one example of that:

You've Got Mail

Dear McKay,

In seventh grade, I was so accustomed to swearing that even misspelling a word by accident would cause me to cuss. I was foolish and called people swear words if I was mad. It never occurred to me that they would feel hurt, angry, or even depressed!

It was a clear, sunny, warm afternoon. I leaped down the stairs, eager to start playing our new Freddi Fish CD rom. What I saw made my blood boil and my heart turn cold. My older sister sat smugly on the big comfy swing chair, her eyes focused on the screen in front of her, her fingers flying over the keyboard. I nicely told her how she was way past her time limit and should stop hogging the PC now. She just glared at me and went back to e-mailing her friends.

Minutes ticked by slowly. I couldn't do anything. She was older, and she was scary.... Slowly, my fear turned into anger. Red, flashing, boiling anger. I had waited ALL DAY to play Freddi, had suffered while being a "good girl," had tried my best to let my parents know that I had a right to play. And then she

came and ruined it all. I was furious and I said two
words that I now regret. "#&%$ you."

I never meant it, it just spilt out. I guess I never
thought about what her feelings might be no matter if
she was hogging the computer or not. What came next
was both unexpected and shocking. My older sister
stared at me for a moment, then burst out crying, flee-
ing from the room to tell my mother, no doubt. Then
it occurred to me that not only did I hurt her feelings,
I also made a reckless and foolish action.

In the end, my mother spanked me and yelled at
me for saying the forbidden curse, and I was grounded
from playing computer for a week. I realized that
swearing did not solve the problem, but only made it
worse.

—Name withheld

This quote proves this even more. This is what P. M. Forni,
co-founder of the Civility Project at Johns Hopkins University said, "Very often, rudeness and cursing are the beginning
of an escalation toward violence. Words, our words, are like
our hands. They can soothe and heal, but they can also strike,
which means they can hurt."

Cussing really does make things worse. It can lead to a
breakdown in so many parts of our lives.

4. Cussing can ruin your opportunities.

At school or work, when playing sports or when running for a
political office, words can affect how you are viewed and what
opportunities are open for you.

Kelly Crabb, the attorney I told you about before, said, "If
I swore like a stable boy in my business, it would affect my

business.… It's just not acceptable for a professional to use that kind of language. It's socially not acceptable."

These next two e-mails show how cussing can ruin your job opportunities and can even cost you money.

You've Got Mail

Dear McKay,

I once interviewed a candidate for a job at the company I worked for. As the interviewer, it was part of my job to try and make a relaxed atmosphere so that the candidate feels comfortable enough to express themselves openly about their qualifications. As this one interview progressed, the candidate began to feel comfortable enough to start using bad language. In my mind, my decision was immediately made. I would not hire her. As she continued to use profanity to color her stories, I wondered why she felt it necessary or even acceptable to use such language. I concluded that cussing was her way of trying to show me her assertiveness. In any case, I was not impressed. If the candidate felt this comfortable with me at an interview, how would she act with our company's clients?

—Name withheld

♦　♦　♦

Dear McKay,

It was a hot summer day. The A/C in my car wasn't working that well. The cars were driving slow in front of me and I was in a hurry. All the sudden, out of nowhere, this guy in an SUV came swerving within inches of my car. OK, maybe not inches but it seemed like it. So, my first reaction was to make an obscene hand gesture and to yell a few other choice words.

Well, you never realize the full consequence of your actions.

I am a real estate agent and I was working with this family to sell their house. I thought that it was a shoo-in on selling it because we were friends at church. Then one day, I drove by their house and noticed a sign from another realtor.

I was shocked that they didn't even say anything to me. Six months had gone by and I was at a church function talking with some friends about the real estate market. A certain person's name came up and I mentioned that I was shocked that they didn't have me sell their home.

The guy who I was talking to said, with a funny look on his face, "You didn't hear?" And, I said, "What?" He said that the reason that family didn't use me to sell their house was because of something I had done six months ago. I said, "What in the world could that have been?" He said he was driving and saw me in the car next to him and swerved, pretending to hit me. He said the next thing that he knew you flipped him off and cussed him out.

So, I learned a lesson. That lesson cost me $15,000 in commissions.

And, more than that, I was extremely embarrassed. This family, my friends, and apparently many people at my church were aware of my foolish actions.

Sometimes in life, you miss out on some of the lessons you could learn because people don't make you aware of your mistakes. I'm glad I had a chance to learn the effects of what a simple thing like our words can have on our lives.

—Anonymous

This next example shows how cussing ruined one person's chance to reach what they felt was one of the most important goals in their life. In a way, it's kind of sad because this guy really changed his life with this one time of cussing.

You've Got Mail

Dear No Cussing Club,

Years ago, while supervising a girls' volleyball game, I noticed a spectator repeatedly throwing something at the backs and heads of the players and coach on the bench. At one point, the coach stood up and looked around, trying to identify the culprit.

I approached the offender from behind and tapped him on the shoulder. When he turned around, I asked him in a calm manner to stop his behavior because it was distracting to the team. I was not loud or rude.

"Who the #$% are you?" he said. "Who in the $%# are you to tell me what to do?"

"I teach at this school," I said evenly, "and I'm supervising tonight. Please stop throwing things at the team or you'll have to leave."

"You can't tell me what to," he said, turning his back on me, "and I'm not leaving."

I walked out of the stands to get help and ran into the [student body] advisor. After I explained the situation, she beckoned him to come down. He complied, and she told him he had to leave.

He leaned into my face, jabbing his finger.

"@%$# you," he said. "I'll get you. @%$# you."

A few days later, the lead campus supervisor told me that the young man had been identified. He'd graduated two years earlier and was a cadet with the Sheriff's Explorer Program. His lifelong goal was to work in law enforcement.

My husband, now retired, was an FBI agent at that time. He knew the deputy who headed the Explorer program, as well as many law enforcement officers in LA and San Diego counties.

He called [the head of the Explorer program] and explained the incident.

"He's done," she said. "We'll take care of it."

—Name withheld

5. Cussing affects your outlook on yourself and the world.

A lot of people seem to start cussing because they want to feel good and look "cool" to others around them. But, after a while, cussing seems to do just the opposite. In e-mail after e-mail people have told me that, rather than feeling "cool," they didn't like themselves as much as before they started cussing. It seems to me that people who cuss don't have as much self-esteem and they start to feel bad about what they do and who they are.

Cussing also changes your views on life and you see more of the negative and the ugly side of life. The great thing is, that can change as you change your language.

See in this example how words made a difference in this woman's life:

You've Got Mail

Dear McKay,

While in school, I came in contact with many who used profanity often to make a point or just out of habit. During this time, I started using the word "hell," thinking that, compared to what some others were saying, that was pretty mild. However, after several months, I noticed my life was becoming a hell … in relationships, homework, and all kinds of things were just not working. One day it just dawned on me that by using the word "hell" so often I had unwittingly accepted that condition as a part of my life. A quote I had heard came to mind: "Your thinking determines your experience." I realized the truth in this and dropped the use of that word from my conversation, and life quickly returned to being joyful and much happier.

With appreciation for all you are doing,

Elaine Dent

These examples show just some of the many consequences that come from cussing. Again, there are some who may think that it shouldn't be that way, that we should all be allowed to say whatever we want and there should never be a punishment or consequence. That may be true, but, instead of expecting people to cut you some slack for cussing, why not look at it in a different way? Think about what you could get for *not* cussing.

Did you watch Michael Phelps in the 2008 Olympics? I loved watching his races and seeing him set all those records and win all those metals. If you remember, some of his races were very close. But, in every case, he was able to pull it off and to win over and over again. Think about what might have happened if Michael had sat back in practice and expected everyone else to just accept him the way he is, without putting in the time and effort to really be the best he could be. Michael Phelps knows that to be a winner you don't change the rules to fit what you want. Instead, you take it up a notch, you do the little things that add up to make a big difference.

I believe the same thing applies to language. We shouldn't expect the rules to change. We shouldn't want cussing to be more acceptable or anything like that. Instead, we can take it up a notch. We can do the little things that will help us avoid cussing and, instead, use language that lifts. I believe that's the way to really be a winner.

Using a
Four-Letter Word

As you can see, I have learned a lot from the e-mails I have gotten in the past two years. But, at first, I didn't know all of those things about cussing and how it can affect you. All I knew, back then in middle school, was that it bothered me and it went against what I thought was the right way to talk.

It actually bothered me more and more all the time. Some days, I would come home from school feeling really down and discouraged—like someone had been beating me up all day. And, really, I think that's true. My friends didn't even realize it, but they were beating me up with their words and it was getting worse every day.

One day, I was totally freaked out about it. I had an extra bad day at school and all the cussing really got to me that day. It was like school just wasn't fun anymore and it wasn't really a place I wanted to be. When I got home, I talked to my mom. I told her, "Everyone at school cusses now, including my best friends."

Mom-type answers

My mom had one of those good mom-type answers. She said, "Maybe you should tell them that it bothers you."

Yeah right! I thought. *You've got to be kidding.*

Moms always come up with crazy stuff like that. You know, like, "Face your worst fears." No way! That may work some-times, but I already felt like a geek. Everybody was cussing. I would lose all my friends for sure if I said it bothered me. I wasn't going to say anything to anybody. I'd just keep it to myself.

That was my plan—to just keep it to myself—and I did a pretty good job of sticking to it. Then, one day, my plan fell apart. My friends and I were all talking at lunch, and every-body around me was cussing. They were laughing and cussing and laughing some more, just being rowdy and out of control. They'd done this before, but this time it really felt like they were looking at me and wondering why I wasn't joining in. I guess everything just hit me at once and I couldn't help it, it just slipped out—a four-letter word: "Stop!"

My four-letter word

Yeah, it's a four-letter word, but not like the kind I was hearing all around me. I totally went against my plan and did what I never thought I would. Ever. Before I could stop myself, I was yelling, "**Stop!** Dude, stop! Do you guys have to cuss **all** the time?"

They all stared at me and my friend, whose nickname is V, said, "What are you talking about, McKay?"

"What do you mean, what am I talking about, V? You guys say the 'F' word in, like, every sentence, dude."

"No, we don't."

"Yes, you do."

"Dude, are you serious?"

"Yeah, I'm serious. Everybody is always cussing and I'm sick of it. I'm trying not to cuss myself and it bothers me when that's all I hear. You can do what you want, but I would appreciate it if you wouldn't cuss around me all the time."

"Okay. Whatever."

That was it. No one said anything for a few seconds and I knew I'd really done it. No more friends. No more hanging out with these guys. It was over. I was going to be one lonely kid.

"Yeah. Whatever." I said.

"Yeah, whatever," V said. "We'll stop cussing if it really bothers you that much."

"What?"

"We'll stop cussing around you, dude. Okay?"

"Oh … really?"

"Yeah. Really."

"Really?"

"What, do we have to take a lie detector test now?"

"No, no. It's cool man…. Thanks."

"Yeah. No problem."

Somehow it seemed too easy, so I still wasn't sure.

I thought, *Maybe there could still be a problem. Maybe they're just saying that to be nice, but our friendship is really over.*

"Dude, thanks!"

I was wrong. Our friendship wasn't over. V and the others meant what they said and we ended up staying friends all through middle school. Then, at the end of the school year, something happened that completely surprised me and, I guess, sort of changed my life. It was just a few weeks before summer vacation, and the next year we would be going to high school. My friends and I were sitting outside at the school lunch tables talking about what it was going to be like. We were wondering if we would still be friends in high school. Would we change? Then, out of nowhere, V looked at me and said, "Dude, thanks."

"What?" I said.

"You know."

"No, I don't, V."

"What you told us."

"What I told you, what?"

"About not cussing and stuff, man!"

"Yeah, McKay, it's because of you that we don't cuss," said another one of my friends.

"I'm a totally different person now," said V. "I don't cuss all the time, and I don't get angry so easy anymore. Thanks, bro!"

The rest of the day, I couldn't stop thinking about what my friends had said to me. It was strange. These guys had been my friends for a long time, but we usually didn't talk like that. I felt totally different for the rest of the day—really good and happy or, like, warm inside or something. It was … you know … cool!

> **Some people say it takes courage to stand up for what you think is right. I think that's true, but I also think you would be surprised to see how easy it can be and what a difference it makes.**

I thought about how my mom had told me to speak up to my friends. What if I hadn't? What if I had never said anything to them? I mean, it wasn't easy to think about speaking up, but, when I finally did, it really wasn't so hard. They hadn't said too much then and it didn't seem like a big deal to them, but maybe it was.

To say something to my friends about cussing was very hard at first. I was so afraid of what they might think that I waited until I couldn't stand it any more. But, when I finally did say something, it wasn't that hard to do and my friends didn't run away from me or treat me any different. Instead, they were glad that I told them how I was feeling and they even thanked me for standing up and saying how I feel about cussing. Maybe their lives were going to be different, in a good way, just because of something I said.

Some people say it takes courage to stand up for what you think is right. I think that's true, but I also think you would be surprised to see how easy it can be and what a difference it makes.

I like the saying, "Stand up for what is right even if you are standing alone."

Are you a little afraid like I was, or, when you see something happening that just doesn't seem right, do you have the courage to stand up and say something?

Here are some things that might help: Think about what it is you are afraid of. Are you worried that people won't like you? Are you worried about your image? Are you afraid you will lose your friends? Or, that someone will be angry with you or will want to get back at you or even hurt you? What are you afraid of?

Someone once said, "Courage doesn't mean the fear is gone, but it means you set aside the fear and take action for the good of yourself or someone else."

Remember the Cowardly Lion in the Wizard of Oz? In the part where Dorothy scolds him, he starts to cry and then says, "You're right, I am a coward! I haven't any courage at all. I even scare myself. Look at the circles under my eyes. I haven't slept in weeks."

Then, the Tin Woodsman asks him, "Why don't you try counting sheep?"

The Cowardly Lion says, "That doesn't do any good. I'm afraid of them."

It wasn't until they got to Oz and the Wizard gave him a Courage Medal, that the Lion saw that he had courage all the

Your Own Badge of Courage

Congratulations!

You probably have more courage than you think!

See if you can answer "yes" to four or more of these questions.

	Yes	No
1. Can you think of a time when you were afraid to do or say something, but you did it anyway?	❏	❏
2. Have you ever had to stand alone for what you think is right?	❏	❏
3. Have you ever tried something new, even though you were afraid at first?	❏	❏
4. Do you keep your language clean and try not to cuss, even when everyone else seems to do it all the time?	❏	❏
5. Do you ignore negative peer pressure when your friends try to get you to do things you don't want to do?	❏	❏

If you answer "yes" to four or more of these questions, you deserve you own Badge of Courage. If not, think about what you need to do to be more courageous next time you need to take a stand. You can do it ... and, you'll be glad you did!

time. He found out that courage doesn't mean you are never afraid, but it does mean that, even though you are afraid, you stand up and do things you believe in.

It's not always an easy thing to do. But, I promise you it's worth it.

5
"Wanna Hang with Us? Don't Cuss"

That day, when my friends thanked me for helping them make the decision to stop cussing, they said something else too, and this is really the thing that got the No Cussing Club started. They said it wasn't easy for them to stop cussing, and they didn't know how to stop at first, but, they said, every time they hung out with me, they remembered that they had promised me they wouldn't cuss.

That was it! All of a sudden, I realized that the thing my friends said had helped them was also something that could help me. If making a promise worked to help my friends stop cussing, that same thing could also work to help keep me from ever getting into the habit of cussing. If I made a promise to my friends that I wouldn't cuss, just seeing them would remind me and would help me keep my promise.

That's when I had the idea for the No Cussing Club.

Making a promise

It just sort of came to me. A No Cussing Club, a club for anyone who wanted to join, would be a way for me and other kids to make a promise and to sort of challenge each other and help each other use clean language.

Then, with all of us together, the club would make it so we had a group. Like, we could fit in without having to cuss just to look "cool" or to have friends. It was so awesome! It would be like peer pressure, but in reverse. Instead of pressure to do something I didn't want to do, my friends would be the positive pressure I needed to keep from cussing. Instead of cussing to fit in, it would now be the "in" thing to not cuss.

Sweet! It was a great idea! What could be more perfect? Or, so I thought, until I told my dad about what I wanted to do.

Are you crazy?

When I told my dad I was thinking of starting a No Cussing Club, he stopped right in the middle of what he was doing and stared at me.

"Are you crazy?" he said.

I really didn't think I was. I thought it was a great idea—until my dad reminded me that all the kids at school may not feel the same way my friends did.

Several months after that, when talking to a news reporter, my dad explained it this way, "I was afraid that McKay would get picked on like no other kid in history. And, not only that, I wasn't sure that he could really change anything. I didn't want him to go through being ridiculed and harassed and then not have any success in getting his club off the ground."

He tried to tell me all those things, but I guess I was just excited about the whole idea of a No Cussing Club. I was excited to think I wouldn't feel left out and different any more. I asked my dad again and kept bugging him about it, but I couldn't make him see it my way.

"But ..."

"No."

"But …"

"No. I don't think it's a good idea."

"But …"

"No. It's a waste of your time and I really think you'll be asking for the kind of trouble that you don't really want."

Well, you know what kids do when they want something and they can't seem to get it from dad—they bring in the "big artillery."

Mom.

I don't know what it was, but, for some reason, my mom went along with the idea. Maybe she didn't know how bad things really were at school. Or, maybe she did know how bad I wanted to try it. Whatever it was, she said she thought I should go for it and that's all it took for my dad to go along with it, too.

> **I realized if I made a promise to my friends that I wouldn't cuss, just seeing them would remind me and would help me keep my promise.**
> **That's when I had the idea for the No Cussing Club.**

During the time I was trying to convince my dad, I was already checking out things at school. Like I said before, it was near the end of the school year, but, still, I went to talk to the principal at my middle school, Mercedes Metz, about my idea of a No Cussing Club and how I thought it could help kids.

She told me that at South Pasadena High School, where I would be going the next year, they had official clubs and that I should try to start the No Cussing Club there. She said that I might want to start getting members for the club at the middle school and then I would have more of a chance of getting approval in high school.

That sounded good to me.

Come and join the
No Cussing Club

YA WANNA HANG WITH US?
DON'T CUSS!

Location _____
Date _____
Time _____
Tel # _____

Parents are invited to come with kids
Receive free T-Shirts and be on our website!

www.nocussing.com

Quit your cussing!

I talked to my dad about some of my ideas for getting members and, now that he was on board, he helped me get started. We made a flyer that said: "Wanna Hang with Us? Don't Cuss." My friends helped pass out the flyers around the middle school. Within two weeks, we had about 25 people who said they wanted to join the No Cussing Club. I couldn't believe it. I had no idea that there would be that many other kids who were willing to take the No Cussing challenge. Sweet!

School ended for the summer and middle school was over, but we had a pretty good start for going into high school and starting the No Cussing Club there. During summer break, I did all the regular summer things, but close to the end of summer, I talked to my dad about how to get things going again. I wanted to make sure we had things ready so we could have a No Cussing Club at the high school.

I invited all the No Cussing Club members and some other friends over to my house for a pizza party. My friends told their friends and tons of people came. Our living room was totally packed. We had made crazy orange T-shirts and official-looking certificates and we passed them out to everyone there. By the end of the party, we had a list of more than 50 kids who wanted to join the No Cussing Club.

I was stoked! But, I was shocked at the same time. This thing was big.

Still, I was a little worried about taking this to the high school. My middle school principal said I needed something official, something that would show the high school that we meant business and that we did deserve to be a club at the school.

The first day of high school was about a month away. What could we do in that time that would make our club look like the real thing?

A Web site

We came up with the idea of putting together a No Cussing Club Web site where people could find out what we were about and could easily join our club. People would be to be able to go onto the Web site and download a certificate (like the one below) to show they were a member or to order a T-shirt if they wanted. Best of all, a Web site would make

it so we could get members from all over, not just from our high school. So, we had my uncle, Cary Inouye, help us create www.NoCussing.com.

The No Cussing Club theme song

Next, we also put together the No Cussing Club theme song. It's called "Don't Cuss" and the first line says, "If you want to be my peer, please respect my ears. Don't cuss!" The theme song tells the story about our club and about the No Cussing challenge.

We got some of the other No Cussing Club members to help with the chorus, then we went around town with a video camera and told people about our club and asked them to say "Don't

cuss." Then, we put this funny video together for our song and posted it on our Web site. Little did we know that within a couple of months, our goofy little song would be heard and viewed hundreds of thousands of times and the song would even end up being broadcast on a Los Angeles radio program hosted by Ryan Seacrest.

Here are the words to the No Cussing Club theme song:

Don't Cuss

I was sitt'n in the schoolyard
Hangin' with my crowd,
When some kids came walking by,
Talkin' really foul.
Every other word
Was burnin' up my ears,
So I took a new stand
And challenged all my peers.

(Chorus)
If you wanna hang with us,
I don't wanna hear ya cuss.
If you wanna hang with us,
I don't wanna hear ya cuss.
Don't cuss! Don't cuss!
If you wanna be my peer,
Please respect my ears.
Don't cuss! Don't cuss!

I was sitt'n in the park,
Talking to my friends
When we heard adults cussin',
I thought, "Man, it never ends!"
I said, I know I'm just a kid,
But I'll challenge you, too!
They said, "Kid, were really sorry,
Can we hang with you?"

(Chorus)

Blankity blank,
Bleepity bleep,
I don't wanna
Hear that speak.

Bloopity bloop,
Yakity Yak,
Stop your cussing,
Clean your act.
Don't cuss! Don't cuss!

My dad was watchin' news,
And I was tryin' to chill
When I heard about the language
On Capitol Hill.
So, I guess I'll write a letter
To my congressman
I'd like to give a challenge
To my government

(Chorus)

All across the nation
We'll start a new sensation
Don't cuss! Don't cuss
Let me restate it,
Keep it G-RATED!
Don't cuss! Don't cuss!

So, we had a Web site, a song, 50 members and crazy orange T-shirts. We couldn't go wrong. We were definitely ready for a high school club.

High school, here we come

It took only about half a day for me to see what my dad had been so worried about when I first talked about starting the

No Cussing Club and for me to start thinking, "Am I crazy or what?"

It was the first day of school and I had already seen what could happen when someone doesn't like what you're doing. It all started out so innocently. I was just walking to lunch, for heaven's sake. How was I to know there were areas that were off limits to freshmen? Senior territory was not labeled anywhere on the school map. I had already heard stories about kids being thrown into trash cans and things like that, but no way was I prepared for what happened next.

All of a sudden, this angry senior lifted me up off the ground and, in one quick motion, slammed me against the brick wall. Then he pinned me against the wall with one arm and started to punch me with the other. I suppose I could have cried or screamed for my mom—after all I was a freshman, you know—but I just closed my eyes and wondered how I was going to get out of that mess. Little did I know that help would come in the form of a girl's voice yelling from the crowd, "Aw, he's just a little guy, leave him alone." Just like that, I was saved. Who says angels don't exist?

Headed for the dumpster

Okay, so while I was glad that I didn't end up in the trash can or that the guy didn't knock my teeth out and waste all that money my parents had paid for braces—I did walk away from that with a sort of sick feeling. Just think, if I was attacked like that for innocently walking into the wrong area of school, what would happen if I started a No Cussing Club? I figured they'd skip right past the trash cans and go straight to the dumpster with me.

I can make a joke about it now, but at the time I was pretty scared and wondered if I should just give up the idea of the No Cussing Club all together.

But, I couldn't forget what my friends had said. It was, like, echoing in my head, "It's because of you, McKay, that we don't cuss." Then, what about the 50 people who had already joined and the e-mails I had already received from kids who felt the same way I did and who thanked me for starting the club back in middle school? I couldn't let them down. They were looking forward to participating in Club Rush.

Club Rush

Oh, man! I had decided not to throw in the towel, but that doesn't mean I liked the idea of club rush. Club rush meant I was going to be standing in the halls at lunchtime, while the whole school walked by on their way to lunch, and I would be wearing an orange T-shirt no less and trying to talk to people, competing with other clubs to get members to join a No Cussing Club.

"Oh yeah, I am crazy," I decided. "I'm definitely going to end up in a trash can!"

But, like it or not, Club Rush was here.

"Hey, everybody! Over here! Be an official member of the No Cussing Club."

"The what?

"The No Cussing Club. Join today and get a free orange T-shirt."

"What the … ?"

I couldn't believe I was really doing this. And, kids were really coming over and checking out my club. *Whoa, look at that! My sister just signed someone up; it really helps to have a sister who's a popular junior. Yeah! Sell it, Ashlyne!*

That's how things started. Things were petty slow, but nothing horrible was happening, so I didn't mind that we weren't signing up a lot of people. Then, along came one of my soccer teammates. This guy is cool. He is the team captain, and he is a senior too! *If he signs up, our club will have instant "street cred!" This is going to be sweet!*

I guess I thought that since this guy knew me and we were teammates, that he would at least listen to what we had to say. Instead of listening to us, he had a lot to say himself, things I can't really repeat in a book about not cussing.

It went something like this: "The No Cussing Club? What a @%$# joke! Look, guys, it's the @%$# No Cussing Club! Oops, I @#%& cussed. $%@$! @&#^%! Ha ha! What a bunch of @#$& nerds!"

Man, was I ever wrong. It didn't matter that we played on the same team and that people looked up to him. He just totally dissed our club!

Right after that, someone else shouted, "@#$% the No Cussing Club."

What could we do? We just stood there in our orange shirts, feeling pretty foolish. In defense, and because we couldn't think of anything else to say, someone from our side spoke out in a little voice, "But, you guys can get your community service hours in our club!"

"@#$% your community service hours," came another voice from the crowd.

Trust me, the trash can was looking really good right about then. More people started cussing at us. Then it was like a feeding frenzy. You know, like when a shark smells blood in the water and starts thrashing around devouring poor, innocent little fish and whatever else they can get their teeth into. All I could think of was, *Ring bell, ring.*

A Word about Bullies

S o, yeah, I guess you could say I was being bullied. I was
getting thrown against a wall by a kid just a few years older
than me and, every day, people were bullying me with their
words. It was like I was being "pushed around," but with words,
not with someone's fist. I guess I was okay with it because I
had a lot of people who were joining my club and I had friends
who believed in what I was doing.

Of course, I was scared sometimes and didn't like it, but I
had seen a lot of kids at school who were bullied much more
than I was, so I didn't think it was too bad. Then, my dad
helped me see it a little differently.

Last year, in my freshman year, I started to play tennis.
I had seen these kids playing, running all over the court, slam-
ming the ball back and forth. They were like pros. I was just
amazed watching them. It was way better than seeing those
tennis matches on TV where everyone's all quiet for the serve
and stuff. They were running all over and just the sound, and
the speed, it was, well, cool.

I've got to try that! I thought.

A couple weeks later, I heard that there was an open spot
on the school team. I tried out and actually made it.

One day, I was practicing at the school courts with my dad when a group of kids walked by and started cussing like crazy at us. My dad told them to knock it off, but they just kept going. My dad started freaking out. I'm thinking, "*Uh oh*." I can see it! Dad's going to go ballistic. These kids have no idea what they're in for. These kids were cussing, my dad was yelling back and I'm running over to tell my dad to let it go. My dad stopped for a second and looked at me. The kids were still cussing at us. I could tell my dad really wanted to tell them off but he looked at me like, "Okay." We just ignored them, walked back to the court and kept playing. They were all just laughing at us until they finally left.

My dad was still way upset. I could tell our fun was over. He said, "That's ridiculous. Who are those kids? I'm going to talk to their parents."

I'm like, "Dad, you have no idea. That was nothing. I get that kind of stuff every day. So, you're going to be talking to a lot of parents."

Being picked on, pushed around, punched, poked, etc.

It's true. I do get that kind of bullying sometimes and a lot of other kids do too. In fact, I have heard about a lot of kids who get picked on or pushed around or punched or poked or put down or—the list goes on, but it all fits under that same category called bullying. It seems one kid bullies the next and then he turns around and bullies someone else and it just keeps going. I've seen some bullying at my school and you've probably seen some at your school too.

A lot of days, I'm just walking down the halls at school and kids "accidentally" bump into me. I can hear kids laughing behind me. I know they're picking on me and making fun of me because of the No Cussing Club. Yeah, I have lots of friends because of it, but I still have some who want to tease and bully me and push me around. When they start doing all this stuff, I just keep walking. I keep looking forward. I pretend it doesn't bother me.

One time my friend was with me when it happened. She was totally shocked. These guys walked up alongside of me and started cussing and saying really disgusting stuff. They pretended like I wasn't even there, like they didn't know I was around. But, it was pretty obvious, especially when, in between the cussing and gross talk, they could hardly control their laughing. Yeah. Very funny.

My friend said, "McKay, I'm so sorry. I had no idea. How do you let that not bother you?"

Want to know a secret? It *does* kind of bother me.

In the beginning, it *really* bothered me. It made me not want to go to school. It made me angry. It made me want to stop doing the No Cussing Club.

Now, I know what's probably going through your head right now. You're probably thinking, *Dude! You brought this on yourself. Your dad told you not to do it. Orange "No Cussing" shirts? What were you thinking? You knew you would get picked on.*

Yeah, I know. It's true. I know that's the big reason people tease me. I know that all I would have to do is stop this whole "No Cussing" thing and the bullying would pretty much go away.

But, I know that's not the case for some kids out there. I get e-mails from kids who are having this happen all the time. They are getting bullied at school and they don't know what to do.

I think about these kids who haven't done anything that should make them get picked on or who haven't given anyone any reason to bully them. If I feel as bad as I do and am all bummed out by the bullying I get, man, I can only imagine what these kids must feel like. I wear an orange T-shirt—I just about ask for it. But, these kids haven't done anything to make people pick on them and they don't know what to do to make it go away.

What is bullying?

The dictionary defines a bully as, "a blustering, quarrelsome, overbearing person who habitually badgers and intimidates smaller or weaker people."

Sounds pretty bad, doesn't it? Well, it is.

A bully is someone who tries to hurt other people, on purpose. They do it to be mean, to make others feel bad or uncomfortable, or to make fun of others.

Bullies may:

+ Get physical, with things like hitting, pushing, poking and pinching.
+ Ignore someone or leave them out of activities.
+ Gossip or tell lies about others.
+ Criticize other kids for the way they dress, their race or, even, a handicap they may have.
+ Intimidate or threaten other kids.
+ Say or write mean things about people, calling them names or using put downs and other verbal abuse, like cussing someone out.

Bullies often will pick on people who are smaller than they are, or who are different in some way. A lot of times bullies do what they do to look "tough" or get attention, but a lot of times it's because they have been bullied at home or at school themselves and bullying someone else is their way of sort of "getting even."

Are you Being Bullied?

Do any of these things happen to you?

If you answer "yes" to even one of these, but, especially if you answer "yes" to more than five, you are most likely being bullied and it's time to get some help, **NOW.**

Follow the suggestions in this chapter to help prevent bullying, plus, **show this list to your parents, your teacher or another adult you can trust and talk to them about what you can do to be safe.**

	Yes	No
1. Do you ever get hit, pushed or punched by other kids?	❏	❏
2. Do kids laugh at you or make fun of the way you talk or the way you look?	❏	❏
3. Do some kids yell at you or cuss you out?	❏	❏
4. Do you sometimes feel afraid to go to school?	❏	❏
5. Do you feel like some kids leave you out or ignore you?	❏	❏
6. Do any of the other kids at school call you names?	❏	❏
7. Do you ever feel like you don't have very many friends?	❏	❏
8. Do you sometimes feel worried or upset or feel like crying when you're at school?	❏	❏
9. Has anyone ever taken anything of yours or damaged any of your things?	❏	❏
10. Do you feel like some kids gang up against you?	❏	❏

Bullying is not funny in any way, shape or form. And, whether you are the one bullying someone, or the one being bullied, it needs to stop. Now. Bullying only leads to more bullying, more sadness and more hurt—and can even turn into more violent acts and more serious results.

If you are being bullied, get some help now before it gets any worse or makes you feel any worse. Here are the best ways to get help.

Tell someone

First, you've got to tell someone. I think, the more people who know, the better. That's what bullies are afraid of.

Do you remember that senior I told you about back at the beginning of the book, the one who was going to punch me out on my first day at high school? Guess what happened to him. He got busted. You know how?

Don't mess with my mom

I told someone. I told my mom. Don't mess with my mom. She went to the school and talked to the principal. That was the end of the bullying in "senior territory." It turns out that that same guy was picking on other kids, too, but I was the first one who spoke up about it.

I was afraid to have my mom go over there. I worried that the principal may let it out who told and then the bullying would be worse. But, all that worrying was really crazy because teachers and principals know about these things. They know about bullying and they know how to handle it. But they can't do anything about it unless they hear that there's a problem.

I went to people who I knew would be on my side. People who had way more power than some "weak sauce" kid at high school. Find an adult who will help you like your mom, dad, teacher, counselor or principal. Get people on your side.

My mom and dad will go to bat every time for me, but I know some kids who don't have a real good relationship with their parents. Their parents are really busy all the time. They might give them some pep speech but it really doesn't help. They're not the kind to go down to the school. In that case, talk to someone at school. Most schools today don't put up with bullying.

At my cousin's school, some kids were picking on one boy. He told the principal. **Boom!** The principal at that school called in all the parents and brought it right out in the open with everybody. That whole thing was over, pronto!

On the other hand, I know another kid who was getting bullied at his school. He told his principal and his principal said that the bully didn't have a "record," so he just gave the bully a warning. Nothing really happened. Then, the kid who was being bullied finally told his mom and she went down to the school to handle the situation. That pretty much ended the whole deal. No more bully.

I think the reality is that you have to tell as many adults as you need to until the situation is handled. The more people you tell the better. Tell your parents, your teachers, your friends, anyone you can think of. Bullies know the only way they can keep bullying kids is if no one finds out. They love to have it kept a secret, because that means they can keep doing it! They will even bully you to keep you from telling someone that they are doing it! Bullies will tell you, "Don't tell anyone." They say that if you tell anyone they will make it worse. Obviously, telling is the worst thing for them, but it's the best thing for you. Tell someone—tell everyone—and the bullying will stop once it's out in the open.

Safety in numbers

Along with telling someone, the second thing to remember is that there is "safety in numbers." When I first started in Boy Scouts, our Scout leaders planned to take us on a hike and an overnight campout. I remember the leaders telling us about some of the rules and some things we needed to do to be safe. The thing I remember most is that they told us, "There is safety in numbers. Don't ever go in the lake or follow a trail by yourself. Always have at least one other person with you."

This same thing applies when it comes to bullying. Be sure to tell adults, but, along with that, you may have a friend or there may be some older kids at your school who will help you.

One day, I came home from school and my dad said that there was a phone call for me from someone at my school. I didn't recognize his name at first, but he knew my name. He was a senior on the varsity basketball team. He had been watching me at school and saw all the flak I was getting. He said that he cussed a lot, but that because of what I was doing he was trying to cut down and he hoped to stop.

Finding a friend

He said some things that really made me feel good and that I have thought about a lot since. His words have given me courage to face a lot of stuff. He said, "I have never seen someone with the kind of drive you have. People are getting down on you because they have never had the kind of passion you have."

I didn't know this guy really well, but I knew he had a lot of friends at school and was pretty respected on campus. He told me that if I ever had a problem at school, I could come see him and he would back me up. Not that he was going to beat up anybody, he said, but if people saw that he was cool with me then they might not give me so much grief. He told me, "Don't give up on what you are doing. Someday it will pay off. Don't give up."

Maybe there are kids like that at your school who will help you out. I'm not saying to create a gang or to go get your friends to bully someone else. Nothing like that. What I am saying, though, is that it can help to let your friends know what's going on. Don't be embarrassed or afraid to talk to other kids about this. Who knows? Maybe one of your friends knows some older kids or has a big brother who would be willing to help you.

Reach out. You have no idea what you might find. If you don't find help right away, don't give up. Trust me.

You may feel all alone and feel like you are some kind of a royal geek if these bullies picked you to pick on. Stop that. Know that something is wrong with them, not you. Reach out to other people. Who knows, there may be someone else who is getting bullied just as much as you and would really like to have a friend to talk to too. While you're looking for help, you may very well be able to help someone else just as much as they will help you.

One group that is trying to help stop school bullying says, school bullying is widespread across the United States. They say that each day 160,000 kids refuse to go to school because they don't want to face the physical and verbal abuse of their peers.

Reach out. You have no idea what you might find. If you don't find help right away, don't give up. Trust me. There is someone out there who will listen and someone who cares. There really is safety in numbers. So, create safety from bullying by expanding your circle of friends and people you care about. Help look out for them, and you'll find those same friendships and caring will come back to you.

I had no idea that anyone at my school cared about what was going on, but then I got that phone call. Just the fact that I knew that there were other kids on my side made me feel tons better.

Are you being a bully?

When I was being bullied at school and having cuss word after cuss word yelled at me, I think one of the worst things was knowing what it felt like to be bullied and then realizing that I had done it too! I wasn't what you would call one of the biggest bullies on the block, but when I became the target of bullying, I realized that there were times I had made fun of people or done other mean things. I guess, like cussing and other bad habits, sometimes you can start being a bully without even knowing you are doing it.

Maybe you have been bullied yourself and you feel you need to strike back. Maybe you don't feel confident, so you think you'll be more cool if you make fun of others. Maybe someone really does bother you or make you mad and you don't know the right way to deal with them. Whatever the reason, bullying is not the answer. It will only lead to more bullying and more misery. Check this out to see how big a bully you may be ... and then, read on, to see how you can make changes.

Are you Being a Bully?

Do you do any of these things or have you done them in the past?

If you answer "yes" to even one of these, but, especially if you answer "yes" to more than five, you are most likely being a bully and it's time to stop, **NOW.**

Follow the suggestions in this chapter to stop bullying, plus, to get some extra help, **show this list to your parents, your teacher or another adult and talk to them about what you can do to stop being a bully.**

	Yes	No
1. Do you ever hit, push or punch other kids or do other things to hurt kids on purpose?	❏	❏
2. Do you laugh at kids who are smaller or different than you or make fun of the way they talk or the way they look?	❏	❏
3. Do you yell or cuss at other kids?	❏	❏
4. Do you like to feel stronger and tougher than other kids, and do you try to make them feel afraid of you?	❏	❏
5. Do you like to make other kids cry or embarrass them?	❏	❏
6. Do you call other kids names?	❏	❏
7. Do you think some kids are not as good as you and deserve to be bullied?	❏	❏
8. Do you gossip about other kids, tell lies about them or try to make others not like them?	❏	❏
9. Have you ever taken or damaged other kids' things?	❏	❏
10. Do you hang out with kids who like to gang up against others?	❏	❏

If you bully others, there are a few things you should know. If you beat up on other kids or bully them in any way, you could be the one who ends up hurting the most. That's because bullies are more likely to drop out of school, more likely to smoke, drink alcohol and get into fights. Bullies are even more likely to commit crimes later in life. So, you see, bullying just isn't the coolest thing to do.

I suggest two things that can help you stop bullying. For me, seeing what it felt like to be bullied made me never want to do that to someone else. So, first, think about what it feels like to be bullied and then decide you won't make anyone feel bad on purpose anymore. Just like when someone wants to stop cussing, if you want to stop bullying, the best thing to do is to make a promise to yourself and to others that you won't do it anymore.

Second, you may want to talk to an adult who can help you. It may not be fun to admit you have been bullying others, but your parents, a teacher or another adult you trust can help you see how to make better choices. Besides, they would rather talk to you about it now, rather than later when you are in big trouble for something you've done.

So I say, stop bullying … and, especially, since cussing is one of the most common ways people use to bully others with words, I say it again—"Don't cuss."

It's Official!

I can say all kinds of stuff about bullying now, but that day during Club Rush, when I was waiting for the bell to ring and put me out of my misery, it seemed like lunch hour lasted way longer than normal and I wondered if the cussing at me and the rude attacks were ever going to end. *Was the bell broken or something?*

"@#$!% the No Cussing Club," yelled someone from the crowd.

"The No Cussing Club is for losers."

"Get your #$!%7*(^% Club out of here."

Okay. Why didn't I just listen to my dad? I thought. *He tried to tell me, but nooooooo, I had to bug him and bug him and bug him.*

(What's wrong with kids these days? Why don't they just listen to their parents?)

It seemed things were completely out of hand, we were being cussed at right and left and we only had a few people who had signed up. And, we still had one more day of Club Rush the next day.

Again? More torture? More humiliation? No way! No way!

By the time I got home, I was exhausted and so tired of being yelled at and cussed out. I really just wanted to tear that orange T-shirt off and never see it again.

You've got mail

I got on the computer to do a report for one of my classes, but I got distracted for a minute when I saw the message, "You've got mail."

I was still kind of in a daze after everything that happened at school, until I read the message that sort of woke me up all over again. The message said:

You've Got Mail

Dear McKay Hatch,

I found your Web site and I think it's so cool. I'm nine years old. My family just moved to Alaska. I don't know anyone here. Everyone on my school bus cusses really bad words. I hate it. I don't know what to do. I'm glad you made this club. I feel like there's someone out there who knows what I'm going through.

—Anonymous

What was I going to tell this kid? Was I supposed to e-mail him back and say, "Hey, deal with it, bro. Don't even try to fight it. This club's a joke and I'm dumping it"?

Not! I knew I had to keep going. Like before when I wanted to quit, I saw what this club could do for kids and knew it was worth it to keep going.

So, there I was the second day, wearing my orange T-shirt again, and trying to smile while I said: "**Step up folks.** Join the No Cussing Club! Get credit for community service hours. Get a free T-shirt."

"@$%^ the No Cussing Club!" someone yelled.

"You guys are idiots!" Cuss. Cuss. Cuss. Cuss.

Here we go again! I thought. *This is totally humiliating. It was weak sauce!*

I got through the day, but when I got home I was even more tired than the day before. I was completely wiped! I felt like all the life had been drained from me. I went to bed at five o'clock in the afternoon and didn't wake up until the next morning.

Then, I had to go to school all over again. But, this time, no Club Rush.

Thank goodness that's over, I thought.

It's official!

But, I soon found it wasn't over. In fact, we had just begun. When I got to school, one of the girls in our club showed me our club roster. We had signed up more than 100 members. I was amazed—more like floored. We had ourselves an official high school club! The official No Cussing Club. The first No Cussing Club ever.

Orange to the extreme

Our club was up and running, but would our orange T-shirts ruin everything? I thought they just might.

The Dreaded Orange T-Shirt

Have you ever heard that bright yellow stuff attracts bees? I don't know if that's true, but I can tell you what bright orange No Cussing Club T-shirts attract. I mean, just picture it ...

A high school freshman ...

stepping out into a crowded hall ...

a bright orange T-shirt ...

big, bold, black letters, with the words:

"Ya Wanna Hang With Us, Don't Cuss!"

Yeah, I was pretty much asking for it—I'd already attracted enough bullying and I was sure to be in for more—and I was encouraging all the No Cussing Club members to do the same thing. I asked them all to wear their orange T-shirts to school every Friday.

My friend was freaking out.

I'm not going to wear it, dude. Look man, joining the club is one thing. I mean its cool and everything. But, DUDE! An orange T-shirt? Every Friday? Let's just put targets on them while we're at it.

The thing is, I understood exactly what my friend was thinking. I was thinking the same things.

But, I was the No Cussing Club president and he was the vice president.

HE was the vice president

Yep, that's right. He was my vice president, and he was the one who was freaking out about the shirts.

But, I was still amazed he was even there at all! **He** was the vice president? I still couldn't believe it.

Remember the soccer team captain who cussed us out—the same guy who was one of the first ones to cuss us out at Club Rush, the same guy who started the cussing frenzy? He was now the vice president. **He** was the vice president of the No Cussing Club.

You would never guess how it all happened.

One day during soccer practice, the team was all running together. I was running along in the middle of the group when, from behind me, I hear, "What's up?" It was the team captain.

I had no idea what was coming, but I didn't figure it was going to be good.

Oh no. Not again. Please don't cuss me out in front of everyone on the team.

"Hey, you're the guy from the No Cussing Club."

"Yeah."

"So … um … I'm sorry I cussed you out, bro."

"What?"

"Hey, all my friends were there that day and, … uh … Well, anyway, I know I shouldn't cuss because my family is religious and everything. We really don't believe in that. So, … sorry. How do I join your club?"

Yep, that's the way it happened. Really.

After that, the whole soccer team was "recruited."

The captain stood in front of the others and said, "Look, I'm the team captain and so whoever cusses on this team or bugs McKay gets punched out. Okay?"

I *think* he was kidding, but I'm still not exactly sure.

Whether he was kidding or not, it worked. And, just like I imagined during Club Rush, having him in the club worked with the other members of the team and with other kids too. Or, something did. I'm not sure what helped most, but with having the soccer team captain as our vice president and with nearly 100 of us wearing those orange shirts every Friday, something was working!

We were getting more members and, wearing the shirts was helping in another way too. Wearing our orange shirts on

Friday reminded us about the promise we had made to not cuss or use bad language.

My brother and sister go orange

Those shirts even got the attention of my younger brothers and sisters. I didn't force them to, or even ask them, really, but my brothers and sisters wanted to support me by wearing orange No Cussing Club T-shirts to their schools too. They were pretty brave about it at first, when they were just talking about it, but then, when it came time to actually wear the shirt, they felt the same kind of fear that I knew well.

"I'm afraid to wear it, Mom," said my little brother, Dakota.

Dakota is two years younger than me and he was in middle school. He's like the nicest kid ever. He wouldn't hurt a fly. Really! We gave him the nickname "Dr. Doolittle" because he is so nice to any animal he's ever around and he always treats people with kindness too.

"You don't have to wear it," my mom told him.

"Yeah, I know; but McKay wears his and he's not afraid."

Yeah right, little bro. I'm not afraid to walk down the halls of my school in the dreaded orange T-shirt. Do you know how many times I've been "accidentally" bumped into?

As Dakota was heading out the door for school wearing the T-shirt of death, he yelled, "Okay! Bye, Mom. If I come back home with a black eye, you'll know why."

Some kids did tease Dakota and gave him all kinds of grief at school that day.

But, Dakota knew how to handle it. When one kid said, "What's the deal with that dumb club and that weird shirt?" Dakota just said, "It's for kids like you who cuss all the time."

He cracks me up!

Yeah, Dakota got hassled, but, by the end of the day, we had a few more kids from his school who wanted to join the club.

Then, there's my younger sister, Saige. She wanted to wear the T-shirt to her elementary school, but when my mom tried to drop her off at school, she wouldn't get out of the car.

"Okay, Saige, have a good day at school," my mom said, but she wouldn't get out.

"What's wrong, Saige?" said my mom.

"I'm afraid they'll laugh at me. I want to go home and change my T-shirt."

"That's fine, sweetie, but then you'll be late for school. You wanted to wear it so badly, why don't you try it for one day and see what happens?"

Mom convinced Saige and she finally got out of the car.

When Saige came home from school that day, her attitude was completely different. She was totally excited. Six of her friends wanted T-shirts and wanted to join the club.

Shirts around the world

Now, we have people in every state and all around the world who have orange T-shirts—or orange No Cussing Club wristbands—that remind them of the No Cussing Challenge and help them stay committed to not cussing.

For example, there's Lynda Hill, from Australia, who sent me this e-mail.

You've Got Mail

Hi, I just joined your elite club and purchased a set of your wristbands! I will wear mine daily to constantly remind me to watch my mouth as the occasional naughty word does slip out. I will also ask my friends and family to wear your wristbands to remind them also to "watch their mouth." I am a lady in my 50s and it's still not too late to learn from the young ones. Good luck to you. I see great things ahead for you. The path you are choosing in life could put you in good stead to become President one day. Remember whatever we do in the past can catch up with us; so, good luck in life.

Kindest regards,

—Lynda Hill
Australia

Taking it to the
Next Level

All the T-shirt wearing and the talking was helping the No Cussing Club grow at school. But, that wasn't all that was happening. Our Web site was constantly changing and being improved and attracting more people all the time. As more and more people were going onto the site and taking the No Cussing Challenge, I was getting more and more e-mail from people saying how the No Cussing Club was making a difference in their lives.

And, the more stories I heard, the more I wanted to reach out even more and help even more people. It seemed, too, that the more the No Cussing Club grew, the more I became aware of cussing going on in other places.

Even people in our government were cussing each other out, like some people in Congress and even the Vice President. It's true. A CNN news story from back in 2004 told about a disagreement between Vice President Dick Cheney and Senator Patrick Leahy. Apparently Vice President Cheney cussed at Senator Leahy. According to the CNN report, when Mr. Cheney was questioned later, the Vice President said, "That's not the kind of language I usually use."

When asked if he had cursed at Leahy, Cheney answered, "Probably."

I'm not saying Mr. Cheney is the only politician who has used bad language. Far from it. There are many other reports of politicians and government officials who curse and use profanity.

There are all kinds of reports about the bad language used by some movie stars and it seems like some athletes think they can't participate in their sport without swearing.

I also had heard about how cussing was getting worse in movies and on television and music, especially music aimed at teenagers, had more cussing than ever.

Studies prove more cussing on TV

I had heard a lot of people say that, that the cussing was getting worse. Then I learned about some studies that proved that was true. A study by Harvard University School of Public Health said, "Violence, sex, and profanity in American movies increased significantly between 1992 and 2003, while ratings became more lenient." Called the Kids Risk Project, the study said, "There was more sexual content in films rated PG, PG-13, and R, which requires children under 17 to be accompanied by a parent or adult guardian. More profanity was used in films rated PG-13 and R." The study also found that even animated movies, meant for kids, were getting worse. "Animation doesn't guarantee appropriate content," the report said.

> You always hear adults telling kids to watch their language, but there are a lot of adults who aren't being good examples to us.... I realized adults needed the No Cussing Club almost as much as kids did.

You always hear adults telling kids to watch their language, but as all these things show, there are a lot of adults who aren't being good examples to us. Some adults are even encouraging us to cuss with the movies and music they are making.

It just didn't seem right and I realized adults needed the No Cussing Club almost as much as kids did.

Write your Congressman

I decided to write a letter to my local congressman, Adam Schiff. Congressman Schiff liked what he heard and what he saw on our Web site. He said he supported us and he actually became an honorary member of our club. We also talked to the sheriff over all of Los Angeles, Sheriff Lee Baca, and he became an honorary member.

Not too long after these two men joined the club, the Los Angeles County Super-visor, Michael Antono-vich, called me and said he wanted me to come down to his office. When we met with him, Mr. Antonovich said he was proud of what we were doing. He shook my hand and said he had something for me. Then, he presented me with an official Letter of Com-mendation from the City of Los Angeles.

The commendation had my name on it, and

it said, "In recognition of dedicated service to the affairs of the community and for the civic pride demonstrated by numerous contributions for the benefit of all the citizens of Los Angeles County."

That sounds like a lot of big words, but I knew what it meant. It meant the No Cussing Club was not only helping kids at my school, but people in all of Los Angeles County.

More than Los Angeles even, the No Cussing Club was beginning to spread around the world. It was awesome to see how it spread. I had told my cousins about the club. They live in Gilbert, Arizona, and they started a chapter of the No Cussing Club there. We told other friends who lived in other parts of the United States and the world—and they told others, and so on.

Making headlines

Then, the No Cussing Club made the headlines of our local newspaper. Bill Glazier, the editor of the *South Pasadena Review*, first broke the story. He heard about what I was doing and he says, "I instantly told myself: 'This is a great story. I hope no one gets to it before I do.'"

Mr. Glazier explains why he was so interested in the story.

"What makes news is something out of the ordinary or something that's not supposed to happen. Planes are not supposed to crash. Homes are not supposed to burn down. People are not supposed to rob banks. All of these are examples of everyday news. When I heard about McKay starting a No Cussing Club, unlike a plan crashing, a home burning down or a bank being robbed, all of which are daily occurrences, I knew this story was something special. It was a first, something I wanted to jump on because I had a sense the story would capture the attention of the media worldwide, and it did. Before writing the first story, I told McKay's father, Brent, that this will be a huge story."

Mr. Glazier says he knew the story would interest a lot of his readers, because, "It's the fact that, seemingly, everyone has cussed at least once their life and it's intriguing—and newsworthy—when someone starts a club where profanity is off limits…. It really doesn't matter how you view the club. Whether you're for or against it, the fact that someone started a No Cussing Club is big news. It's new, unique and different. By the large number of people who have joined the No Cussing Club in recent years, it's evident that many believe there are better choices when selecting words to communicate."

It was great to have the attention from this reporter and to know he liked the idea of the No Cussing Club and what we were doing. But, he also said some nice things about me.

He told people, "I've always admired McKay's enthusiasm and commitment to make the No Cussing Club a huge success. He's never wavered and has handled the naysayers, those who oppose his cause, with the same respect and dignity of those who support him. It's wonderful to watch McKay grow up and handle all his success so well. He's a remarkable young man."

That was nice of Mr. Glazier to say so, but I'll tell you what was remarkable.

People were signing up for the No Cussing Club from all over, taking the challenge and

downloading certificates of their own. We soon had members in 10 states, then 15, then 25.

What if we could have members in every state? I wondered.

More to do

Yes, the club was growing, but, still, we wanted to do more. It seemed the more we grew, the more e-mails kept coming in about the cussing people were hearing in public and in front of their children. These people wanted to see things change and they were, like, asking for our help.

Here's an example of one of those e-mails:

You've Got Mail!

It was a sunny day at one of the popular amusement parks in Southern California. My wife, my 10-year-old son and I were enjoying an outdoor show, when suddenly a flurry of obscenities filled the air around us. I expected to turn and see a group of teenagers sitting behind us. Instead, I discovered a young father with his wife and daughter (four or five years old) settling in for the show a couple of rows behind us. Not only was there profanity in every sentence the man uttered, but the subject of his conversation was completely inappropriate for this family setting. My frustration began to build as I'm sure it did with all the other people around us. As a factory operations manager and former U.S. Navy officer, I usually have no problem confronting people. But in addition to this guy's language, his demeanor suggested that our confrontation would be a long one, possibly physical, ending up in the parking lot and on the evening news. I had to make a quick decision; risk ruining the rest of the day for my family and I, or bite my tongue for the last 15 minutes of the show. Let's just say that my tongue was sore for the rest of the day. I'm sure there were a lot of sore tongues that day.

More than the fact that he used this language in front of his young daughter, I marveled at his inability to discern the discord between the setting and his language. A year later, I am still conflicted over my decision to sit there stewing with the combination of the wonderful entertainment being performed in front of me to the sounds of profanity in the background. Part of my inaction was a result of today's sad culture where youth seem to take a simple rebuke to the extreme of a physical confrontation that ends up on the news. But did my inaction also contribute to this man's inability to consider his language in a crowded family setting? If I had spoken up, would there have been others to back me up? Could I have taught this guy a lesson?

Tim Norris
Castaic, California

At one of our No Cussing Club meetings at the high school we brainstormed ideas for what we could do to raise awareness for using better language. As we talked about this, one club member told about his dad and how much cussing he heard at work, but also outside of work and around kids, like at ballgames and the movie theaters. Several club members said they had heard their moms and dads talking about the cussing they heard near the playground, at the local park, at soccer games, near the library, and at other places where kids are always around.

It's a sign

Then, one of the kids at the meeting told us about a picture they had seen online. It was a picture of a sign that is posted on the boardwalks in Virginia Beach, Virginia. It is a funny sign, meant to remind people to watch their language in public, because there might be kids around. That gave us an idea. Wouldn't it be cool if our city would do something like they did in Virginia Beach and put up signs at parks and other places where there are a lot of kids?

We all agreed that it would be cool, but how do you ask your city to do something like that? Somebody mentioned that they heard about a meeting the city has every month where anyone can go and talk to the mayor about things they would like to see happen in the city. The meeting is called a City Council meeting and most cities have these meetings and allow citizens to speak at them. We found out you have to sign up and then they give you about three minutes to say whatever you want. So, I signed up to talk about the signs, and to ask the city if they would create what we called "No Cussing Zones."

No Cussing Zone

About 15 club members went with me and we all showed up in our orange T-shirts for the City Council meeting. There were a lot of other people there. The mayor and all the City Council members were there and there were all these other people who wanted to say stuff too. One guy stood up and talked about fixing holes in the roads. Someone else used their time to talk about making safer crosswalks. Finally, it was my turn. I was shaking inside. I was hoping no one could see how nervous I was.

When I stood up, I said, "I have lived in this city my whole life. I really like living here because it feels like a small town, even though we are between all these big cities. I like how people seem to care about where we live."

Then, I said, "I remember, one time, they were planning to build a huge freeway—the 710—right through the middle of our little city. That would have pretty much been the end of this city. The freeway developers even bought a bunch of people's homes and, to this day, that street is like a ghost town. I remember when they were trying to get the freeway approved. It was right around the time of the Fourth of July parade. Everybody in our town goes to the parade every year. I have been in it many times for my school, our Scout troop and other stuff. That year, the best part was when this guy was dressed up like a bill that had the freeway name, '710,' on it. Another guy was dressed up like a stamp that said, 'VETO,' and he chased the '710' guy up and down the parade. Everybody was going nuts—screaming, whistling and clapping. It was cool because we felt like we saved our little city."

"I still remember that because it made me feel good to know people in our city would work together like that," I said. "It taught me that if you believe in something, no matter how small you are, you should fight for it. I believe in something that I think is worth fighting for. I believe too many kids are cussing now, because they hear adults doing it. I hope we can show what kind of city we are and that we care about kids by creating 'No Cussing Zones' in different places in the city."

When I sat down, the mayor and the City Council members clapped and thanked me for my words.

Cameras rolling

I walked out of the meeting, and there were these guys from the news there with TV cameras. Whoa! They asked me all kinds of questions about our club and about how we were trying to "ban cussing."

Those questions taught me a lot. I was beginning to see more and more how people see things differently and how you have to be careful with the words you use. Our idea wasn't to "ban cussing" or to force anyone to stop cussing. It wasn't like we were trying to pass a law so the police would arrest anyone who, like, smashed their toe and accidentally said a swear word. It wasn't like that at all. We just wanted to see if the city would put up signs as a reminder that, hey, there might be kids around, so be careful with the way you're talking.

That night after the City Council meeting, when the local news came on, there we were. The No Cussing Club had made the local news. It was funny to see myself and our No Cussing Club on TV and we all laughed about it. Then, someone called us and said we had been on another channel, and then another, and another. Whoa! That was pretty cool!

Well, the city didn't go for our idea—they said they couldn't force private businesses to put up signs like that and, even for city parks and other places run by the city, they would need people to vote and approve such signs. So, our idea was shot down—but we had our day at City Hall.

Flood of e-mails

Later that night, my dad called me over to the computer and said, "Check this out." Bleep, bleep, bleep, bleep, "You have a new message," "You have a new message"… The e-mail was going nuts! The messages just kept coming in. All night long, e-mails were coming in. We figured the only explanation was that the news clip was being shown on other channels across the United States.

We were so stoked to know people were hearing about the No Cussing Club. The word was getting out! The problem, though, is that many of the words that were coming back in were not what we wanted to hear. Along with all the good and positive e-mails, we had hundreds, even thousands, of e-mails like this:

"@#$% you, McKay."

"Who the @#$% do you think you are?"

"%$#@ your No Cussing Club!"

It was like Club Rush all over again, but, this time, I was getting cussed out by adults too. I mean, you always think adults are the ones telling kids to watch their language, but now, the second a kid was telling them to watch what they say, here were adults that were getting all tweaked out and even angry.

Some of the e-mails were just filled with swear words and nothing else. Others were like verbal attacks. They called me all kinds of bad stuff. They said all kinds of disgusting things about me and my family.

It was freaky to be getting all these e-mails from random people who I had never even met, from people who had just seen me on TV, but who were so angry and had so much hate for me. I thought it was really weird. I mean, I was just a kid in South Pasadena who started a club with his friends. I wasn't forcing anyone to join or anything like that. But, for whatever reason, my speaking out against cussing and bad language made some people really mad.

Some even threatened me. They said they wanted to find me and hurt me and even said I should be killed. When these kinds of e-mails first started coming in, my dad began screening the e-mails for me and deleting the really horrible ones. But, now, when the e-mails turned violent and when my dad answered the phone one day and it was a death threat aimed at me, my dad didn't mess around.

Call in the FBI

He went to the police. The police told him that because this was dealing with e-mail, that it was something the FBI would need to look into. The police contacted the FBI and those guys were totally awesome! I have a whole new respect for them and what they do. They actually tracked down some of the worst e-mails and found they came from an adult in Florida.

Even with these negative things going on, the positive e-mails also poured in. They came from all over and we were getting new members from all around the United States.

A couple of days after we were on television the first time, we got a call from FOX News. They wanted us to go to their studio in Los Angeles for a live interview with their news host, Shepard Smith, who was in New York. They sent a limo to our house at five o'clock the next morning. A limo! Sweet! The studio didn't look anything like what I expected. It was just like a big warehouse, with this fake-looking stage where we sat for the interview. Oh, and they put makeup all over my face. Gross! We were all hooked up with microphones and earpieces and the camera guy said, "You're on."

I heard Shepard Smith say, "Today we're here with McKay Hatch, founder of the No Cussing Club." It was so cool. He totally supported our idea of raising awareness for people to use better language. He was tripped out that I was getting death threats over a No Cussing Club, but he said that there would always be weirdos like that out there.

The whole thing was like a big blur. It was over so fast and the next thing I knew, the limo was dropping us off at home.

We got up so early and all the excitement and stuff kind of wore me out, so I just wanted to go to bed. But then my dad came screaming out of his room, "McKay, the e-mail is going nuts again." The computer just kept beeping to tell us we were getting mail again. This time, it looked like big chucks of e-mails were coming in at once. We were getting hit with thousands of e-mails. There was still a lot of bad stuff, but we were getting tons of messages from people who said they liked what we were doing and wanted to join. We were getting people signing up from countries all around the world. Then all of a sudden …

"Error message"

The e-mail crashed. Our Web site couldn't handle all the e-mail we were getting, so it errored out. We had to upgrade our site to handle all the mail.

The following week, I was on TV again with MSNBC. The day after that, my cousin called us. "Dude!" he was yelling over the phone, "Ryan Seacrest just played your 'Don't Cuss' song on KIISFM all over Los Angeles."

Like I said, the e-mails were coming in every day; most were positive, and my dad kept screening and deleting the ones that were full of cuss words. We also were getting more people who were actually calling our house too. They were calling at all hours of the night. At first my dad would answer the phone, but the calls that came late at night were just people cussing us out. So he ended up just pulling the cord out of the wall.

Have You Ever Been Owned?

"We got owned! We just got owned!"

I had no idea what my dad was talking about. I could tell he was totally upset, but I didn't have a clue what it meant to be "owned." I had never heard of it, but I could tell my dad's whole mood had changed from just a few minutes earlier.

We were at Disneyland. Our family and uncle Cary and his family were staying at a hotel nearby. Dad and uncle Cary kept being goofy and saying, "Tower of Terror! Tower of Terror!" They were playing around, trying to get some of the kids to go on the Tower of Terror ride the next day with them but no one wanted to go. It looked way too scary. I had broken my arm a few weeks earlier at soccer practice. So I had a legit excuse! Going to Disneyland with a broken arm is totally lame, you can't go on any of the cool rides, but I was still looking forward to being at Disneyland the next day. We were all up late that night going back and forth between our room and our cousins'. That's where I was when my dad came in saying, "We got owned!"

At first I thought he was playing, still trying to get us to go on the ride, but he wasn't making sense. "We got owned"? What was he talking about?

Dad told me it meant our No Cussing Club Web site had gotten hacked into or "owned" by some very disgusting people who put all kinds of pornography on it so when you went to our site, all you saw was this sick stuff.

Now I knew how it felt to be owned. It was sick and disgusting. There was nothing we could do. My dad was trying to remove the stuff, but nothing was working. All of our work was ruined.

How could this happen? How did they hack in to our protected site? Protected? Yeah, sure. What we learned from this was a really scary lesson. We found out it is so easy for these guys who know something about computers to hack into any site. All you can do to be safe from them is to watch your site all the time and to have tons of backups in case you need to pull it down and start over.

My dad was on the phone all night long with the Web site support guys. Finally, he said we had no other choice.

"Shut it down," he said.

This Site Under Construction

Freedom of speech

So I learned what "owned" meant and I started to understand about another kind of bullying, the kind that is done over the Internet, with people trying to hurt you or make you feel bad through e-mails or "owning" your Web site. They even have a name for this kind of bullying. It's called cyberbulling.

We'll talk about cyberbulling in the next chapter. For now, let me just say it seemed like every day was adding to my "research" and giving me lots to think about. The phone was ringing all night long. People were calling and cussing out my dad until he disconnected the phone. Our e-mail was flooded with tons of hate e-mails. Our Web site was hacked into and had pornography all over it. People were posting disgusting things on YouTube and in blogs that slammed me and everything I was doing. Someone had threatened to kill me. We had to call in the FBI.

I couldn't believe it. We were under attack by some kind of army. They had control of everything. At least it seemed like that sometimes. But, there were a lot of things they couldn't control. My family, my friends and other club members continued to stand by me. We were getting more attention from schools and from the media and all of it was positive, all of it encouraged me to keep going.

Speaking at the
Muslim American Society convention

I remember one time when that encouragement was really helpful. It's kind of funny now, but at the time it was a serious and pretty scary situation.

Let me give you a little background, my mom and dad, Brent and Phelecia Hatch, are great parents and they have always been examples to other parents. They were named Parents of the Year in 2001 and they wrote a book called *Raising a G-Rated Family in an X-Rated World.*

My mom and dad often are asked to speak at parenting conferences and things like that.

Well, about the time things were really heating up with the No Cussing Club, my mom and dad were asked to speak at the Muslim American Society convention in Los Angeles. It was a parenting convention, but they were also holding some classes for teenagers. The organizers of the convention asked my mom and dad to bring some of us kids with them. My brother and sister were going to do a part of the presentation and the convention organizers asked me to speak as well. They wanted me to talk about the No Cussing Club and how it got started.

Now, picture this, here we are arriving at a nice hotel, but like some other places in Los Angeles, the surrounding area—like the place we parked—didn't look all that safe to me. There we were, all dressed in bright orange No Cussing Club T-shirts and riding in the crazy-looking van that has a picture of my mom and dad's book and "G-Rated Family" all over the side. It was like a moving billboard advertising that a bunch of geeks were on board. We couldn't have done a better job of looking like an easy target. It was almost like we were asking to be harassed and run out of the neighborhood.

When we pulled up to park, a group of rough looking guys were just standing around, hanging out all over the sidewalk—and staring at us like we were from outer space. A couple more guys were standing in the parking lot right by where we had to walk to get to the front door. To me, they looked even bigger and more intimidating than the others. We piled out of the van and I was sure the orange T-shirts were glowing even brighter than normal! I don't remember ever being so nervous in my life. We walked into the foyer of the hotel, looking like a whole glowing pumpkin patch of Hatches. Inside, there were more guys—who knows where all these guys came from or what they might do. I felt like we were in some sort of geek parade and I was pretty sure they didn't want us parading around them. I know, you're not supposed to think every person is out to get you, but I was already nervous about talking to the convention and this just made me more nervous than ever. They stared at us and I felt like they were moving in closer, just waiting for a chance to jump on their prey.

Show time

I was miserable. We had to wait in the foyer about 10 minutes and it felt like about 10 hours. Then, it was time to go down the hall to where we were going to be speaking. I wanted to walk, but my legs wouldn't move. I was sort of numb and, well, just afraid. All of a sudden, this group of young kids who were waiting for the convention to start walked by and as soon as they saw us and our shirts, they started singing the No Cussing Club theme song. They had already gone onto the No Cussing Club Web site and had learned the song on their own. That was so cool! I just stopped and stared at them for a minute. It was so amazing to me to think that these kids already were on board and interested in what I was going to say, even before they met me!

These kids kept chanting the song as they followed us down the hallway. My mom had a great big grin on her face and my dad even gave me a high five. Just a few minutes before, I had wanted to burn my orange T-shirt. But now, I felt like I was glowing inside and out and it felt great. Those kids and their singing totally changed my mood. I forgot all about the fear I felt when we first got to the hotel and it seemed like all the frustration from the past few weeks disappeared too. All the stuff that had happened, all the negative stuff, just sort of went away.

An hour or so later, when I stood up to give my talk, I felt a little nervous for just a second. There were tons of people in the room and most of them were adults. But then, I looked over to one side and saw a bunch of kids. I remembered them singing and I felt good all over again. I gave my talk—all about the No Cussing Club—and didn't feel scared at all. It felt like I was talking to a room filled with my friends.

That one experience really showed me how we were helping people and making a difference, even with people I didn't know.

Then, on top of that, all the positive e-mails we were getting helped me see that even more. Almost every day, and even several times a day, we heard from people who told us things like this:

You've Got Mail

Dear McKay:

I was introduced to the No Cussing Club by the media coverage earlier this year. I am pleased when anyone takes a public stance against profanity, vulgarity and other foul language. I have been encouraging others to speak up for clean language for years. One story in particular stands out in my memory.

In 1998 I stood in the checkout lane at a grocery store with my daughter who was six years old at the time. Two teenaged girls filed in line behind us as one of them carried on a conversation at a volume loud enough for everyone around to hear. Both the topic and the words she was repeatedly using were filthy. You could almost sense the uneasiness of the other customers around as she spoke. I was amazed that the most that anyone managed to do was glance disapprovingly in her direction. She never even noticed.

After a few seconds of this, I turned and said, "Please watch your language."

She immediately snapped, "Mind your own business." Her voice dripped with contempt.

I replied firmly, "This is my six-year-old daughter. When you talk like that in public and around her it is my business. Apparently no one around you has taught you to mind what you say, so I'll do it for them. Watch your language."

She had nothing else to say. Everyone else in line heard me, but only looked away quickly. Almost a minute later another teenager who had just finished paying for her items came back to me and said, "Excuse me." I expected a lecture about minding my own business.

Instead she said, "Thank you for what you said. The language at my school is terrible. If more people would say something, maybe it wouldn't be so bad."

After telling that story a few times, one of my friends gave me the nickname "Captain Decency." Through the years I have experienced great response from people when asked to simply show respect for my family by cleaning up their language. I'd like to think that there are more decent people out there who would be willing to expect clean language and politely require it, especially in public.

> —Matthew Trill
> Clearwater, FL

Cyberblying

So, I'd been owned, blasted with hate e-mails, slammed on blogs and YouTube and even threatened over the Internet. It's hard to imagine that someone could bully you through your computer, but, as I was learning, it happens. Lately, I've heard about it in the news a few times and this is something that is happening more all the time.

Some of the news reports even tell about some terrible things that have happened because of cyberbullying, and some people have even been arrested for bullying people over the Internet. One woman from Missouri was charged with "conspiracy to cause emotional distress and illegal use of computers" because she harassed a 13-year-old girl through MySpace.

Cyberbullying is on the rise

I found this from the National Crime Prevention Council. They said: "An increasing number of youth are being victimized in a nontraditional method commonly referred to as *cyberbullying* or *e-bullying*. In 2004, half of 3,000 U.S. youth surveyed stated that they or someone they knew had been victims or perpetrators of cyberbullying. Teens are using e-mailing, instant messaging, text messaging, and defamatory personal Web sites to threaten, embarrass, and ostracize their peers."

Wow! Half of the youth in the United States said they had experienced cyberbullying. And that was back in 2004. I'm sure it's even more now.

I learned about cyberbullying firsthand, before I really even heard that word or knew that people were doing it. It was a frightening experience and, like I said in the beginning of the book, to those people who tell me, "Words don't mean anything," I say, "You're wrong." When it's coming through your computer, it's all words. And those words certainly meant something to me.

Dad takes on the cyberbullies

When the No Cussing Club was in the news the first time, I was getting slammed with all kinds of e-mails that were filled with hate, cuss words and threats. But, guess what. After the first few e-mails like that, I never read any more of those e-mails. My dad did. He read everything before I did, and still does. He would tell me how he couldn't believe the garbage people would send to a 14-year-old kid.

He read me a couple that weren't too bad (substituting "blankety-blank" where he needed to) and it wasn't just the cuss words that bothered me. It was also the whole sound of the e-mails. They sounded like they were full of hate and anger.

So, even though my dad read everything, I did have some idea of what was coming in and just the thought that all these people were cussing me out and sending me all this negative stuff made me feel down. Just like the bullies at school, these cyberbullies were trying to make make me feel bad and to hurt me—on purpose. And, in a way, it was working. After a couple of weeks, I felt like there was this, like, this black cloud over me or something. I just felt down and yucky. It was really bothering me. My dad said that he could feel it too. At one point, he decided that he shouldn't read the e-mails anymore because it was affecting us so badly.

It's really weird, because 50 positive e-mails would come in and then we'd get one negative e-mail and that one negative e-mail would sort of ruin things for a while. It would just change our whole mood. We would keep going over that one e-mail in our mind. Then, sometimes, my dad and I might even talk with other members of the family about one of the e-mails or we might talk about it at the dinner table and then my family would all feel negative too.

> **Cyberbullies sort of invade your personal space. They show up on your computer, in your home, where you aren't expecting it at all, and, all of a sudden, you feel like there's this strange negative force all around you.**

Sometimes a message would make us mad. We would want to say something back that would prove our point or defend ourselves. At first, my dad did send a few e-mails back, but that never worked. They would just send even more garbage. We realized that they weren't interested in seeing where we were coming from or having a discussion, all they wanted was to insult us, get us down and make us feel bad. They were just being bullies—and, really, I think these are bullies of the worst kind because they can hide behind their computers and you never really do see who is doing the bullying. They sort of invade your personal space. They show up on your computer, in your home, where you aren't expecting it at all, and, all of a sudden, you feel like there's this strange negative force all around you.

Taking a break

My dad stopped reading the e-mails for a while. We just sort of needed some time away from them. We talked about shifting the focus from all the negative stuff people were saying about us, so we could get back to focusing only on the positive things about our club. We just wanted to keep it fun. We decided not to focus on the negative stuff anymore. Just talking about it and making that decision really worked. The dark feeling went away.

A few weeks later, my dad went back to the e-mails. As soon as he opened any messages that had cuss words or any of that garbage, he just deleted them without reading the whole thing. We focused on the e-mails that were upbeat. We had plenty of those, all kinds of e-mails from people who said that the club was really a positive thing in their lives. By focusing on the positive, it almost seemed like the others went away. Negative e-mails were still coming in, but we quickly got rid of them, didn't let them affect us and went on to those that were positive. By doing that, the whole feeling seemed to change. It was great. We could see so much more about how we were helping people and what the No Cussing Club means in their lives. That's what we try to focus on now.

The effects of cyberbullying

I can see how some people are affected by cyberbullying. When someone is e-mailing you stuff, you feel like you want to read it. If it shows up in your e-mail, you feel like it's something meant for you. So, you open it, not knowing whether it's positive or negative. Once it's open, you may be slammed with all kinds of junk before you even know what hit you. You read it once, and almost can't believe what you read, so you want to read it over again to see if maybe you misunderstood it. You sit there sort of in shock, not sure quite how to take it. You want to defend yourself, so you write back.

Here's where some people make a big mistake. We learned how important it is to back away from these guys. Don't get caught in their game. The only thing they are after is to mess you up. You only have one **real** defense. Turn it off. Shut your computer down and walk away. Whether it's by e-mail or in one of the sites like MySpace or in a chat rooms or on a blog or whatever, someone can only bully you if you're on your computer. There are too many weirdos out there on the Internet, so just stay away from it.

There actually is another side to this and it's kind of crazy that I have to bring this up, but I will say one thing about participating in cyberbullying. There are a lot of companies out there trying to find ways to cut back on the cyberbullying that goes on and, like I said before, there are even arrests being made. Still, there are a lot of kids who are getting in trouble and even being hurt by online predators because they don't walk away from the cyberbullying. And, more and more kids are participating in this and becoming cyberbullies themselves. This is especially true for girls. In fact, one study found that twice as many girls as boys had bullied someone online.

Here's what one company that studies cyberbullying says about it, "Instead of whispering a rumor to a friend, a bully might e-mail or instant message that rumor or post it on the Internet for everyone to see! Or the bully might use technology to ignore you. An example of this would be a friend all of a sudden ignoring your e-mails or instant messages."

I know it may seem harmless and it may be something you think you can get away with. But there really is nothing harmless about hurting someone else. Besides, once you get started doing any type of cyberbullying, you leave yourself wide open

Are you a Cyberbully?

Take this quiz to see. If you answer yes to one or more of these questions, you have participated in cyber-bullying. Read about how to stop and what you can do if you are being cyberbullied in this chapter.

	Yes	No
1. Have you ever sent a mean or threatening e-mail to someone you know or even someone you don't know?	❑	❑
2. Have you left a friend out of a chat room discussion or ignored instant messages from a friend?	❑	❑
3. Have you e-mailed a rumor or gossip about someone to several other friends?	❑	❑
4. Have you posted a negative comment about someone on a blog or a social net-working site (like MySpace or Facebook)?	❑	❑
5. Have you ever cussed at someone or called them names in an e-mail?	❑	❑

for the same thing to happen to you. Why would you want to be involved in a constant stream of online putdowns and harassment? To me this is like what they call a "cheap shot" in basketball, sort of like hitting someone when you think the referee won't see and then running on down the court. What does that really get you? Even if you end up winning, don't you always have to watch your back for someone who is going to do the same thing—or worse—to you? Why would you want to be involved in that kind of stuff?

Like I said above, the best thing to do is to walk away from your computer. If you are the one being bullied, or if you have tried cyberbullying, walk away. That's the best thing you can do and the thing that will protect you in the long rung. Here are a few other tips that will help you stay out of those bullying "rings" and may help protect you from cyberbullying:

Safety Tips for Avoiding Cyberbullying

* Walk away! Limit your time on the computer, especially the time you spend in chat rooms or social sites.
* Don't give out personal information online, ever. That includes your phone number, your real name, or your address.
* Don't tell anyone your passwords, even your friends.
* Never open e-mails from someone you don't know or from someone you know is a bully.
* If you have friends or know people who are being cyberbullies, don't join in! Again, the best solution is to walk away.
* If someone sends a mean or threatening message, don't respond. Save it and show it to a trusted adult.

That last suggestion in the list above is important. Just like with bullying at school, remember to tell someone what's going on! Tell, tell, tell as many people as you can if you ever have someone try to get away with cyberbullying. Remember, telling is the thing that will protect you best. Telling is the thing that will stop bullies cold.

A "Cuss Free" Week

Once we figured out that the best thing was to ignore the cyberbullying and all the e-mails with cussing and rude remarks, it wasn't too long before we were back to our original plan of focusing on the good things and trying to spread the word about the No Cussing Club. Even the arguments we heard seemed to help us see how important it was to keep

going—no matter what other ups and downs were ahead on the roller coaster.

All these things made us realize we needed to do an even better job of helping people understand. It was all about creating awareness.

We got our Web site back up and we went back to the drawing board to see if we could come up with something that would help increase awareness in our city. We wanted to see if we could come up with something the city could back us up on, that wouldn't involve private business or other regulations.

Cuss Free Week

One day, when I was thinking about what we could do, I thought, *You know, if people could just not cuss for one week, just one week, I think they would see a difference in their lives. And, if they could go one week, then maybe they would go two or three.*

So, we came up with the idea of creating a "Cuss Free Week" and of encouraging people to try to stop cussing for that week. We talked to the mayor and the City Council to see if the city would support an awareness week. Our mayor, Michael Cacciotti, really liked our club and the basic idea of what we were trying to do.

Mayor Cacciotti said, "McKay and his friends had come to the City Council to see if we wanted to get involved and we said, 'We really do. This is really important.'"

"We thought how we could best support him and, at the same time, acknowledge his and his friends' efforts would be by proclamation, declaring a whole week, 'No Cussing Week.'"

They discussed it at a City Council meeting and the proclamation was approved. The mayor called to ask me to come to the next City Council meeting and they would present me with the official proclamation.

"We thought this was a way to get people to stop for a moment in their busy lives and reexamine their actions and what they say," the mayor said.

A bunch of club members went to the meeting with me. We were all dressed in our orange T-shirts and had some orange balloons with us. The mayor talked about the club and gave me the proclamation. It looked all fancy and had a gold seal on it and it said:

City of South Pasadena Proclamation

Declaring March 3–7, 2008 as "No Cussing Week" in the City of South Pasadena

WHEREAS, In 2007, 14 year old Mckay Hatch founded the No Cussing Club in his junior high school where students accepted his "No Cussing" challenge and the club was immediately joined by 50 members, and

WHEREAS, through the No Cussing challenge, we could use the positive peer pressure on our friends and if our friends could say "No" to cussing it would be easier for them to say "No" to drugs and violence and

WHEREAS, by supporting and reminding each other not to cuss, the challenge spread around the school and the community and the No Cussing Club membership grew to 10,000 members nationwide, and

WHEREAS, within a month, the No Cussing Club was endorsed by Los Angeles County Supervisor Michael D. Antonovich and joined by the Los Angeles County Sheriff Lee Baca, United States Congressman Adam Schiff and its membership continued to grow and joined by children from 49 states and children from the countries of Argentina, Australia, Austria, Canada, France, Germany, India, Indonesia, Italy, Israel, Japan, Mexico, New Zealand, Nigeria, Philippines, Spain, Saudi Arabia, Scotland, South Korea, and the United Kingdom; and

WHEREAS, the No Cussing Club Founder, McKay Hatch, has been interviewed from radio to television and newspapers spreading the No Cussing Challenge and encouraging the use of clean language which is a sign of intelligence and respect that will uplift, encourage, and motivate-leaving people better than you found them.

Now, THEREFORE, I, Michael A. Cacciotti, Mayor, on behalf of the City Council of South Pasadena, by virtue of the authority vested in me by the City of South Pasadena, do hereby proclaim March 3-7, 2008 as "No Cussing Week" in the City of South Pasadena, California.

Schools get involved

The proclamation was dated March 5, 2008, and was signed by Michael A. Cacciotti, Mayor. When my middle school principal heard about the proclamation, she was really excited about how far we had taken the club. She said she would be happy to get behind the city's "Cuss Free Week" and would encourage students at the middle school to pay attention to their language that week.

Time to Get our ORANGE on!

It was definitely time to get our **orange** on!

As it turned out, all the schools in our city got behind us for "Cuss Free Week." They announced it at school and even put it on their marquees out in front of the schools. The South Pasadena paper ran an article, and it was all over the news again! We got calls from newspapers and from television and radio shows from all over. This time, instead of just hearing the song on Ryan Seacrest's radio show, I actually got a phone call from him, inviting me to be on the show and talk about our club on KIISFM in Los Angeles. *The Early Show* called and *Good Morning America* called as well.

Then, another news story hit that made our story even bigger. It's funny, but the timing of all this was perfect. That very week, two 18-year-old girls had been kicked off a Southwest airplane because they cussed out the flight attendants. Their story was a hot news topic and all kinds of people in the media were talking about it. Some said that these girls had freedom of speech and should have been allowed to fly. Others said that the airplane was private property and that Southwest had a right to refuse service to them. It was weird because our story and this story about cussing were both in the news at the same time and we were talking about some of those same things. Then, we got a phone call that brought the two stories together. The call was from the producer of the *Dr. Phil Show*. That's right, **the** *Dr. Phil Show*. The producer said those girls were suing Southwest, so they were going to have them on their show. They wanted us to be on the same show to talk about the No Cussing Club.

Orange explosion covers the world

Meeting Dr. Phil and being on his show was another of the "ups" on the roller coaster. But, the cool thing is, there really hasn't been a "down" since then.

After the *Dr. Phil Show,* the e-mails from our Web site came pouring in again. Oh, yeah, some of them were still those kinds we really could have done without. And, we still were hearing about blog postings that really ripped me and the No Cussing Club, but it seemed

Photo courtesy of CBS Television Distribution

like those things were easier to ignore knowing how much good we were doing.

This thing had literally exploded and now, like my dad says, it almost had a life of its own. I didn't have to be standing in the hallways at school hoping someone would talk to me and maybe join the club. I didn't have to feel left out at school or like I needed to beg someone to think about their language and how they were talking. All that seemed to be happening without any work from me. Other people had joined in and were talking about the No Cussing Club. Celebrities were beginning to hear about it, like when my sister, Ashlyne, had her picture taken with Hulk Hogan and told him about my club. Community leaders, teachers and church leaders were interested in what the No Cussing Club was doing and wanted to help spread the word.

More than 20,000 members

We had grown to 20,000 members! We had reached our goal to have members in every one of the 50 states in the United States, and we had members in more than two dozen countries, including Africa, Argentina, Australia, Austria, Botswana, Canada, China, France, Germany, India, Indonesia, Italy, Israel, Japan, Mexico, New Zealand, Nigeria, the Philippines, Russia, Spain, Saudi Arabia, Scotland, South Korea, and the United Kingdom.

Some people were still mad. They still cussed me out. Some still said that our cause was pointless. They still said that we were stepping on their freedom of speech. None of that bothered me any more. I knew what we stood for, and I was seeing the good that was coming out of this club.

You've Got Mail

Dear McKay,

   I often walk down the high school hallways hearing every swear word imaginable, and even though it is not right, I question them as a person. Hearing those strong words come out of their mouths, and the immaturity that it puts on them amazes me. I do not swear, and I have always been against it.

   One day my mom and I were watching TV and I soon found the No Cussing Club. I immediately went to my computer and looked up the videos and the

Web site. I was so inspired by the determination of the club that I immediately signed up. Before the No Cussing Club came, I thought that I was alone, and the only teenager that was so against swearing.

When I am frustrated and have lost faith in my friends, I see the No Cussing Club and I know that there are just as many people out there like me that are facing the same struggles. It is amazing how a few words can change a person, and allow them to see the different sides of things. I just hope that nobody gives up on what they believe in, because they are not alone. Thanks to the No Cussing Club I realized that I have support.

—Maddy Herrholtz

♦ ♦ ♦

Dear McKay,

I commend you for your brave actions. Not many people are willing to stand up to friends and peers, especially at your age, when social acceptance plays a vital role.

… When you hear a conversation that is so heavily diluted with vulgarity and cuss words, the power of those words also becomes diluted. Take the monkey house at the zoo, when you first walk in, you say, "Oh, wow! What is that horrible smell?" After 30 minutes, you start to get used to the foul smell and you start saying, "Okay, this isn't too bad." Then after an hour, you don't even notice it anymore, but anyone just walking into the monkey house is saying, "Oh, wow! What is that horrible smell?"

... I guess my point is that your club seems to be on the right track: You want to treat people with respect because it's the way you would like to be treated in return. After all, that is the Golden Rule, you can't go wrong with that.

—Name withheld

My family has always had this saying that we sort of try to live by. The saying is: "Leave People Better Than You Found Them." From the first day we started this club, I used this for our motto. We have gotten hundreds of e-mails that prove we are doing just that. We've gotten e-mails from people saying how happy they feel about what we were doing and that it has given them some kind of hope. They say they feel greater hope for the next generation, hope for their kids, hope that they could make a positive change within themselves. If we have helped just one person out there, then everything that we went through has been worth it. It's nice to think we've accomplished the goal to "Leave People Better Than You Found Them."

Give Me 12 Liberty

So, let's take a step back for a minute. When I first started all this, I knew I didn't want to cuss and I had learned from my parents, my Scout leader and some of my teachers at school that it wasn't respectful to cuss. But with all the e-mails from people and all the questions from news reporters, I had to learn even more and think about what my stand on some things really was. One of the things I learned about was what freedom of speech really means.

One day, I was grocery shopping with my mom. We were at the checkout stand bagging our groceries. There was this kid in line behind us, and as we were walking away with our groceries, he said to the cashier, "That's the kid who's trying to take away everybody's freedom of speech."

That wasn't the first time I had heard a comment like that about "freedom of speech." Kids at school had asked me, "What about my freedom of speech, dude?" Adults said that I was trying to take away their "right to cuss." People were really mad. Someone told me that soldiers had died to protect our freedom to cuss. They said that our nation's Founding Fathers protected our right to cuss in the First Amendment to the Constitution.

"The No Cussing Club is a direct assault on our freedom of speech!" someone said.

Huh?

Just the fact that someone could make that statement seems to show that their freedom of speech wasn't assaulted at all. They obviously could say just about anything they wanted, just like a few others that accused me of interfering with freedom of speech.

Going against the Constitution?

Every time someone brought up freedom of speech, I didn't know what to say. Those statements always made me wonder about **my** freedom of speech and whether **they** were trying to interfere with that. But, at the same time, they were getting to me a little and I started to wonder, *Am I really doing something against the Constitution?*

Man, was I really going against what people had died for just by trying to get my friends to stop saying the "F" word all the time?

This freedom of speech thing really made me think. Maybe I had gone too far with all this stuff. I didn't want to take away anyone's rights.

So, I read the First Amendment. It says:

> Congress shall make no law respecting an establishment of religion, or prohibiting the free exercise thereof; or abridging the freedom of speech, or of the press; or the right of the people peaceably to assemble, and to petition the government for a redress of grievances.

I started asking people what they knew about the First Amendment and about freedom of speech. I found out that people have many different ideas about what it means. A lot of people say that it's basically the right to say whatever we want. Then someone else reminded me that freedom of speech doesn't mean that you have the right to yell, "Fire" in a crowded building that isn't on fire. You can't threaten someone's safety. There are also laws against hate speech.

Kelly Crabb, the lawyer and friend of our family I wrote about earlier, said, "It is true that people can say what they want. There is a free speech right in the United States. However, this right is basically between a person and the government and the government can enact laws in certain circumstances. One of the easy ones is that the government can prohibit a person from making a false claim that there's an emergency."

He also says, "There are also valid restraints on free speech in the context of public settings, for example in school or on television. There have been several very famous cases decided about the use of certain words, which would be cuss words. Basically, the Supreme Court has held and there are laws under the United States that certain words that are deemed obscene cannot be said on television during certain hours."

"If they are a public carrier they have to monitor their speech," he says.

So, the First Amendment of the Constitution does **not** protect speech or expression that is considered obscene. One of the most famous court cases about this is called Miller vs. California. The case was tried in 1973 and today judges still use what is called "The Miller Test," to decide if something should be labeled "obscene." Those things that meet this test and are "obscene" are not protected speech, which means the Constitution doesn't give people the right to this kind of speech.

I was starting to understand a little better about the Constitution and our First Amendment rights, and then this e-mail helped a lot.

You've Got Mail

Dear McKay,

I wanted to say something about all the noise concerning the "Right to Free Speech." The Founding Fathers discussed this subject at length.

They had rebelled against the church because the church fathers were telling them how to think and also they rebelled against the English government telling the colonists how to think and how to live and how to Govern ... and all of the Founding Fathers wanted to assure that the American citizen could freely express IDEAS. It was the area of IDEAS that were protected, your right and MY right to express our ideas. It is called "Freedom of Speech."

Educated speaking is our goal; gutter language lowers us, degrades our dignity, makes us appear ignorant and HURTS others. THE FOUNDING FATHERS DID NOT WISH TO PROTECT A RIGHT TO BE LOW CLASS OR TO HURT OTHERS.

Yours,

Christopher Dupont
Fairview, North Dakota

This made a lot of sense. The Founding Fathers were wanting to be sure that we could speak out against the government without getting in trouble; they wanted to be sure we could express our own ideas without the government telling us how to think.

The reporter I told you about before, Bill Glazier, said it this way: "The beauty of living in the United States is that people will always have their First Amendment rights. Some may be opposed to McKay's actions, but that's to be expected.

In America people are entitled to their opinion and can express it freely. Like those who are opposed to the No Cussing Club, McKay is simply exercising his freedom of speech, which is protected by the United States Constitution."

Then, one day, my uncle was at our house visiting with my mom and dad. I asked what he thought about all this. His thoughts taught me a lot.

"McKay, what our Founding Fathers were fighting for at the time had nothing to do with a desire to protect foul language. I'm really concerned about these e-mails you're receiving and what I'm reading on the Internet. If people don't understand the source of the freedoms that have made our country great, then we run the risk of altering them into something of lesser value."

> "Here's the point, our freedoms should allow us the opportunities to rise higher and do better, reaching for the very best in mankind. Let's hope they are not simply used as excuses to stoop lower into the base, angry, hateful, lustful part of mankind."
> —Cary Inouye

"I don't believe that anyone died with the specific thought that he was sacrificing his life so that we could all go around saying the 'F' word. The mere suggestion of that seems to cheapen their sacrifice. Here's the point, our freedoms should allow us the opportunities to rise higher and do better, reaching for the very best in mankind. Let's hope they are not simply used as excuses to stoop lower into the base, angry, hateful, lustful part of mankind."

My uncle Cary went on to say, "The reason people are fighting against you is because you are calling into question the use of their self-control. Is it being used for the benefit or the degradation of the society which gives them their freedoms?"

"What you, a 14-year-old boy, have started in this country, is a great discussion about the real meaning of freedom of speech. And, that is why I think you should keep going with your No Cussing Club."

So, what is this *real* meaning of freedom my uncle was referring to?

When he said that, it made me remember the many e-mails I had gotten about this. Many of them did come across as angry and hateful. They did seem to be making excuses. They didn't seem to want to do anything to benefit me or society, or to make themselves better.

Eat your vegetables

Yes, I was telling people, "Don't cuss." But, was that suggestion a lot different than if I had said, "Eat your vegetables"? There was no force involved, there was nothing that would interfere with their right to choose. (And, really, when it comes down to it, both suggestions would be good for you!)

Michael Cacciotti, the mayor of South Pasadena, has been a soccer coach for many years. Like me, he could have been accused of interfering with First Amendment rights because he has always been very strict with his players when it comes to cussing and says he believes in taking such a stand.

"When I coach, one of the rules on the field, is that we don't use profanity, even in practice. If you do, you're down for 10 pushups," he said.

Mayor Cacciotti said this rule promotes civility and respect. He says more of us should think about how our actions affect others.

He said, "Every one of our actions or our comments has an impact on someone, whether it's your family or your friends or people important to you, or somebody just hearing your conversation. The impact of profanity, or even a loud voice, causes maybe anxiety, stress, anxiety, or defensiveness.

"We should treat others the way we want to be treated. I don't think …well, there *may* be some people, I don't know … but I don't think many people enjoy profanity or being cussed out."

I got it now. Cussing is not protected speech. Originally, the idea of "freedom of speech" was only to protect people's ability to express their complaints to the government, yet so many people in our society think that "freedom of speech" means you can say anything, anywhere at anytime. Based on the e-mails we get, most young people and many adults are not really aware of the issues and of what freedom of speech really means. I sure didn't understand it at first either.

Now, I know, the No Cussing Club is not going against the Constitution. It isn't interfering with rights or trying to take away anyone's freedom. Instead, with the No Cussing Club and all the things I do to promote it, I am using my freedom of speech to ask others to use theirs responsibly.

How Do **13** I Stop?

The great thing about all this is that people are using those freedoms I was talking about. People all over the world have made the choice to be cuss free! So many people have come to me with amazing stories and they have let me know how avoiding cussing or stopping that habit has changed their lives. I've also had many e-mails that are almost cries for help from people who find they have started cussing and don't know how to turn that around. In one way or another, I've had hundreds of e-mails asking, "How do I stop cussing?"

You've Got Mail

Dear McKay,

I need to stop. It's an addiction. Thanks for your help.

—Anonymous

Many people tell me that using bad language has become a total habit for them. Some say they picked it up without even knowing. They heard it from home, from people they worked with or just from television and movies. Others said they started cussing to fit in or be cool, just like so many of my friends did back in middle school. But now, these people were seeing cussing as a habit they didn't like and something they wanted to change. And, they were asking me how to do that!

I didn't have a lot of answers at first, I could only think to share some of the things I did to keep from cussing. But, since I had never had a cussing habit, I wasn't sure what I could say to really help. Then I realized that cussing is like any other habit you want to break or area you want to improve. I realized I had lots of those, so I did know more about it than I thought.

So I had some ideas, then, I started getting ideas from other people who e-mailed me about how they stopped cussing. We started putting those together and sharing them with others and now, here are the Top Ten Tips that have worked for me with other habits and that other people say work great to stop cussing.

Top Ten Tips to Stop Cussing

1. Realize it's bad.

2. Find a role model.

3. Consider your friends.

4. Use money as a motivation.

5. Use substitutes in place of cuss words.

6. Monitor what you watch.

7. Monitor your music.

8. Get off the Internet.

9. Practice saying positive things.

10. Take the No Cussing Challenge.

So, let's talk about each of these tips and see how you can use them to clean up your language.

1. Realize it's bad.

I think the first step to stop any bad habit, and especially cussing, is to understand its negative effects. I once heard a saying by the well-known author and teacher, Steven Covey, that went like this: "While we are free to choose our actions, we are not free to choose the consequences of our actions." If you truly understand how something can negatively affect you, then you will have the desire to eliminate it from your life. The stories back in Chapter 3 of this book really show how a cussing habit can have negative effects on your life.

Some try to avoid those consequences or say they shouldn't be, but think about it this way: I have a neighbor who plants zucchini every year. And, every time he plants zucchini seeds, he gets zucchini squash. He doesn't get yellow squash or spaghetti squash or any of those other kinds of squash that I don't know because they're kind of sick and I wouldn't eat them anyway. The point is, we do "reap what we sow." And, the sooner we start seeing the consequences of cussing, the more we will want to avoid it or to stop it. Cussing seeds just grow bad cussing weeds.

2. Find a role model.

Having a role model will give you motivation to keep doing better and working toward your goal. If you are only around people who cuss and that is all you hear all day, it may be hard to think of someone who could be a role model. Trust me, they're out there. It could be your mom or your dad, a pastor, or a good friend. It could be a teacher or a coach. Start looking around you and find someone who will be a good example to you.

My older sister, Chari, was a really great role model for me. Like me, Chari saw a lot of cussing at school and she didn't like it and didn't want to cuss. I remember the stories she used to tell me of how some kids would treat her at school and how hard it was for her sometimes. But she had made a choice and I never saw her give in to peer pressure.

When she was in high school, one of her friends would always ask her why she didn't cuss. I guess it was like a totally new concept to this girl that some people didn't cuss. She couldn't stand that my sister never said any bad words. Some of the girls in my sister's class would tease her because she didn't do "freak dancing" at the school dances and she didn't cuss. They said they felt like my sister was trying to be a little "Miss Goody Two Shoes" and that she was trying to be better than everybody else. One girl wouldn't let it go. She would bug my sister every day in science class. "Why don't you cuss? Just say one little cuss word. Come on. Say the 'F' word."

Finally, after this had gone on day after day, my sister asked her, "Why don't you try to **not** cuss?" That question really surprised the girl. She had never looked at it that way before.

A year later, while my sister was away at college, that girl from her science class was walking by our house one day. She stopped and talked with my mom for a little while. I don't think she knew that my mom was aware of what had happened in high school. She told my mom that she really liked Chari and was so impressed with how she held to her standards and didn't let peer pressure get to her.

My sister's example helps me. Knowing she could do it helps me know I can do it too and gives me strength to keep going with what I believe in.

So, I encourage you to do the same. Find a role model—or two or three—find someone you can look up to and who sets a good example for you.

3. Consider your friends.

I think friends are one of the biggest influences in your life. It can be a difficult decision, but, sometimes, if you really want to make a change in your life, you might have to consider who you are hanging out with.

You've Got Mail

Dear McKay,

In seventh grade, I picked up cussing from some of my friends (ironically, at a Christian school). As my life began to snowball into exactly what I never wanted it to become, my language got more and more foul. It seemed that nearly every other word out of my mouth was a cuss word!

Fast forward a couple years to cross country practice in my freshman year in high school. As I was running with a few of my teammates, we came upon another runner who was in middle school. I was no doubt saying something awfully foul when this middle school student said something to me I will never forget. He said, "Why do you have to cuss all the time? You used to be a good kid." This cut me very deeply and was a major catalyst that sent me on the journey to not only cleaning up my mouth, but my life as well. It wasn't easy either.

The first thing I had to do was change who I hung around with. I began to hang out with a group of guys at my school who I knew did not put other people down for what they said. I still had a foul mouth, but it began to get better. Soon, in order to help keep me from cussing, I started paying a new friend of mine, Bradley, a fee of 25 cents for every time I cussed around him.

Fast forward again, now, three years later. While I am still not perfect, I do live a life free from profanity and strive to build others up around me with every word that comes out of my mouth. I realized that truly, every word and action has an immeasurable affect on the world around us. Thank you, No Cussing Club, and thank you, McKay and the Hatch family, for striving to make this world a better place for all of us to live in. Your efforts are truly inspiring! "Never grow weary in doing good, for we will reap, in time, if we do not give up."

God bless,

Tyler Bianco

Another thing about friends is this: I try to have a few different groups of friends that I hang with. I think that is important in reducing peer pressure on you. I have friends at school, friends on the soccer team, friends at church, and friends in my family. That way there isn't, like, a huge influence from just one group of friends. I know if things get too intense with one group or if they start doing things I don't want to do, I can always go hang out with some of my other friends. This way, I feel less pressure to do what they do all the time.

4. Use money as a motivation.

Like Tyler said in the e-mail he shared above, money can be a good motivation. So, set up your own system to help you. Tyler had a system so he had to pay every time he cussed. Notice that he also had a friend who kept the jar, so it wasn't just the money, but Tyler had to face his friend too, who helped him remember and helped keep him in line.

A lot of people say paying for every cuss word they say really works for them. But you could do it the other way around too. You could set up a reward system. Think about something you have really been wanting, or just think about going out for your favorite fast food as a reward. Then, every day you go without cussing, give yourself a quarter, or 50 cents or a dollar. (You may want to set it up too so if you slip you have to take some money out.) Anyway, set the money aside and when you have enough, go get that thing you were saving for or that favorite food—and while you're enjoying it, think about how great it feels to be Cuss Free!

Give it a try.

You've Got Mail

Dear McKay,

I am excited to be in your No Cussing Club. I am a father of five, three girls and two boys. I am 53 years old and this is how my story goes.

I live on the island of Guam with my youngest son Chad and my daughter-in-law, Chrissy. One night I was doing things in my room when Chrissy yelled out, "Hey Dad, would you like to stop cussing with me? It was kind of just an out of the blue question, but I thought for a second and replied back "Sure, why not? I guess that would be a good change," so we started talking about the rules and said that every time we used a cuss word we would have to put 25 cents a jar, but instead we found an empty Gucci candle box and decided to put the money in it, instead of a jar.

We also made an honesty rule that even if we were not around each other that we would have to still count the times we cussed and come home and put the quarters in the Gucci box. We asked our friends if they would like to play along with us, but they cuss so much they did not want to take the challenge. Chrissy and I knew that this would be a good thing for us and did it on our own.

She would come home and say, "Hey Dad, how much do you owe Gucci today?" I would be honest too and I would tell her how much and I would go put the money in the box. It was a lot of fun too and we would laugh each time we would catch each other cussing. Sometimes we would catch each other saying half a cuss word but we agreed even that would count. At times, our friends would catch us and laugh about it because they would see us put our money in the box. This has been going on now for a couple weeks and it is very surprising that people have noticed that we speak with more manners and very rarely cuss anymore. It really does feel good not to cuss because that was one good thing that we controlled about ourselves, and it makes us feel that we are better people because of it.

Thanks for having me in your club.

Your friend,

Wayne

5. Use substitutes in place of cuss words.

Okay, I'm going to talk about using substitutes—words that you can use in place of cuss words. I can hear it now, so bear with me and don't go all philosophical on me. I know some people have a problem with substitute words. I'll just be straight … I don't. People tell me, "Hey, it's basically the same thing."

Come on, folks. Get serious. If you say "flippity flop" all day long at work, is your boss going to say something? Well, maybe he will. Maybe he'll laugh at you. But, if you go around saying the real "F" word all day, you're going to have a problem. What if you're a waitress and you accidentally spill some water on a customer and you say, "Oh, shoot, I'm sorry"? But, what if you spilled the water and said a real cuss word? There's a difference, people. So, if using substitutes is the way you are going to take a baby step. I'm all for it.

Flip! Shoot! Dang! They're all cool in my book. My fav is "weak sauce!" Example: "Bro, that is such weak sauce!"

Look, if you don't have a problem with cussing, then there's no need to start using substitutes. In fact, I wouldn't suggest it because if you start using substitutes you may soon graduate to bigger and not-better words. But, if you are cussing and you're dropping "F" bombs all over the place, then by all means, replace them with "Flip" bombs. From what many people have told me, substitutes can work very well as a baby step and a way to clean up your language gradually.

6. Monitor what you watch.

I heard a saying once: "Garbage in equals garbage out." The stuff that comes out of us—our words and our actions—are the result of what has gone into us. We have to control what goes in if we want to have good things come out. TV and movies are a huge influence on a lot of kids.

TV has so many influences and they are not always good ones. There is not only stuff with bad words, but stuff that makes you angry. There is stuff that makes you sarcastic and stuff that gives you less respect for other people. They are always showing kids bagging on their parents and their parents never do anything about it.

One day I told someone I didn't like all the cussing on TV and they said, "I don't think it's any worse now than it ever was." Well, I decided to find out.

I found out that a study back in 1990, showed that during prime time TV, you could hear a cuss word every 12 minutes. Then, by 1994 cussing on TV increased so people watching prime time television would hear a cuss word every 8 minutes.

Today, it's even worse. There's this group called the Parents Television Council and they do all these studies about TV and other stuff. They looked at all the broadcast networks—ABC, CBS, NBC, FOX, WB and UPN—for two weeks in 1998, and then again in 2000 and in 2002.

The group said that over that time profanity increased on every network and in every time slot. During what is supposed to be "family hour," from 8 to 9 p.m., they found foul language increased by more than 94 percent between 1998 and 2002. And profanity went up by 109 percent during the 9 p.m. hour. That's huge and sickening.

Parents Television Council says the more cussing is heard on television the more it seems like "acceptable language," so they came out against the TV industry and said they need to "get serious" about reducing the cussing on television.

The same goes for movies and videos. Researchers from the Kids Risk Project at the Harvard School of Public Health (HSPH) said that, "Today's movies contain significantly more violence, sex, and profanity on average than movies of the same rating a decade ago."

Significantly more.

So, how do you ever watch a movie or video without taking garbage in when there is so much of it in movies? There are two Web sites you can use to check movies and see what kind of content and language they have. See Kids-in-Mind (www.Kids-in-Mind.com) and Screen It! (www.ScreenIt.com).

And, back to watching TV. How do you avoid hearing all the cussing on TV? I really don't watch that much TV, and I think that's the real trick. I'm not going to purposely let negative stuff into my life, so I just try to stay away and to do other things instead. When I do watch TV, if something comes up that is bad, I just turn it off. My mom and dad taught me that. I have seen them turn off the TV when there is something that they don't like, so it kind of gave me the same power. It may not be easy to do if you're in the middle of an interesting show, but try it. You'll be amazed at how good—and how powerful—it makes you feel to control what you take in.

Remember, "Garbage in, garbage out."

7. Monitor your music.

Music is another story all together for me. I can leave TV alone and it doesn't bother me that much, but I love music. I listen to it all the time.

I don't even have to begin telling you that music today is full of cuss words and music videos, well, we won't even go there. As all kids know, there is a lot of music out there with bad language and you know how powerful music can be. How many times do you find yourself singing a tune and can't get it out of your head? How many times do you sing a line to a song that you didn't even realize you knew? The music has that kind of power to help drive words into our heads … and, then, they have a tendency to stay there.

Music is so powerful. Music can really pump me up, but it can also tear people down with the bad messages, the cussing, the violence, and all the other stuff that is in music today. It makes me a little sad, really, that people take such a powerful and wonderful thing and use it to get their gross and disgusting messages across.

With music, the parental advisory thing works for me. When I see that advisory, I pretty much know it means that they are going to use bad words and talk about nasty stuff. So avoid that song or CD. Again, just like choosing the TV I watch, I try to choose music that lifts me. I'm not going to let some other fool's ideas creep into my head just because he's got a cool groove. There are, like, billions of cool songs out there that I can listen to without having to take in that garbage.

8. Get off the Internet.

Whoa! Some may think the Internet is almost like TV and music, but it **so isn't.** I seriously think the Internet is the worst place for a kid to spend too much time. An article by Daniel Weiss, called "Youth and the Internet" found on the Focus on the Family Web site, says, "Teens are increasingly plugged into the online universe. Their online behaviors range from innocuous research and Web surfing to more high-risk activities, such as meeting strangers, creating multiple identities, and keeping secrets from their parents about what they do online."

His article says 92 percent of teenagers (ages 15 to 17) go online and more than half of those "wired" teens go online at least once a day.

People say that there is a lot of good stuff on the Internet for homework and reports and you just have to be careful. Yeah, yeah. It is **so easy** for kids to get to places where there is unbelievable stuff going on. My advice. Use it for homework when mom and dad are around and then get out of there and go play soccer!

I do want to say one other thing about the Internet. Some kids don't understand the power of the Internet. They don't really get why parents are so concerned. Please don't just blow this off if you are having a problem and are going to those sites or listening to stuff that you know is not good for you. If you are doing that, it may be very hard to stop. Such things are addictive and before we even know we have a problem, we can be stuck. If you're there, remember there is help available. Get some help—then go play soccer!

9. Practice saying positive things.

A great way to stop cussing and keep from doing it is to replace the negative things you say with positive things. Think about it. You can't really say two things at once, so why not just make sure it's the good stuff that you're saying instead of the bad.

One of the coolest things I ever heard was this story about a farmer who couldn't figure out how to keep out the weeds after he harvested his crops. He came up with a really cool solution. He planted flowers! The flowers kept the weeds down and when it was time to plant crops again, it was much easier to get rid of the flowers than it would have been to get rid of weeds.

The same thing can work for the way we talk. The motto in the No Cussing Club is "Leave People Better Than You Found Them." If you're saying positive things all the time, it's really going to sound strange when you say bad words. If you focus on using language that lifts, you'll be more motivated not to cuss at or diss someone with the words you use.

A great way to start this is just by giving a compliment to someone. It might not come naturally to you, so you will have to kind of force yourself at first. Make a goal of passing out at least one compliment a day. And, then, hey, what about this—after you make it a habit of complimenting your friends and family members, how about complimenting yourself for "Leaving people better than you found them!" and for finding a great way to conquer the cussing habit?

10. Take the No Cussing Challenge.

Remember how much power came from the promises my friends in middle school had made? They told me they weren't going to cuss and then it was that promise that kept them going. Whenever they saw me, they remembered that they had promised not to cuss around me. When they told me that, it made me realize the power of making a promise. I didn't want to start cussing, so I made the same promise to them so it would help me not to cuss. What you basically need is to make a verbal commitment to yourself and to someone else, which will help make your promise even stronger and constantly remind you. That was the whole point of the No Cussing Club in the first place. And, that is what we have continued to do through our Web site and through other chapters across the country. On our Web site, we have the following challenge:

The No Cussing Club Challenge

I won't cuss, swear, use bad language, or tell dirty jokes. Clean language is a sign of intelligence and always demands respect.
I will use my language to uplift, encourage, and motivate.
I will Leave People Better Than I Found Them!

By taking this challenge, you will have something to refer back to whenever you need to get pumped up again. From the Web site, you can even print out a certificate to put on your wall as a reminder. Or you may want to get a T-shirt or a No Cussing Club wristband—whatever it takes to help

you keep your promise to yourself. You may even want to consider starting a No Cussing Club chapter of your own. This is such a fun and cool way to have that added support. I give you some ideas to do that in Chapter 15 of this book.

One last thing, I know that cussing can be a hard habit to break for many people. Many of our No Cussing Club members say that they slip up sometimes, but that they're glad that there is such a thing as the No Cussing Club that helps them stay committed.

I truly believe that if you take this challenge, and work hard to stick with it, the only effect it will have is to make your life better.

I wish you the best!

Language that Lifts

Many experts say that the only way to really stop a bad habit, is to replace it with a good one. For example, instead of eating candy, have a piece of fruit. So, don't just stop cussing, start lifting! We've talked a lot about cussing and about the type of language that insults or puts people down. But, while I've been trying to point out what is negative about all that, I don't want you to think this book is all negative!

There's another kind of language that I want to be sure I talk about. Like I've said more than once in this book, words do have meaning and the words we use can tear people down or they can build people up.

When I spoke up to my friends and challenged them to change their language, one of the main reasons was because what they were saying made me feel just sort of yucky all the time. It was like constantly being hit in the face. It didn't make me feel good about my friends to hear them cussing all the time. And it didn't make me feel good about myself even to be around that all the time.

Since starting the No Cussing Club, I have seen what a difference language can make. I have been invited to speak at different schools and community groups and, whenever I give a presentation, I talk about "Language that Lifts."

Use language to make great things happen around you

Instead of using words to hurt others and tear them down, and instead of using our language in a way that makes us look childish and uncaring or even unintelligent, words can be an amazing tool for creating friendships and for making great thing happen all around us.

> "You can gain more friends by building people up than you can by tearing them down."
> —Actress, Sasha Azevedo

I know, I know, it may sound a little sweet and flowery, but it's not that at all. Words are power. Words can open doors and words can change lives.

So, instead of using words that would ruin your opportunities and relationships, there are all kinds of ways to use language to lift—to lift others around you and yourself too.

Here's what I mean: The actress Sasha Azevedo said, "You can gain more friends by building people up than you can by tearing them down. And, you can gain more friends by taking a few minutes from each day to do something kind for someone, whether it be a friend or a complete stranger. What a difference one person can make."

Another quote says, "Being kind to others is the best way to be good to yourself."

How to use language to lift others

Here are some easy things you can do to start using language in a kinder and more powerful way. The following are some simple ideas for using language that lifts. I suggest you try one or two, then come back and try another. I promise that you will see amazing things happen as you start to use language that lifts.

1. Give someone a compliment.

Compliments are great ways to "Leave People Better Than You Found Them." We talked about compliments earlier and said that complimenting others could help you stop cussing. That's just one of the things the compliments can do. Compliments are contagious. Give someone a compliment and you'll see their face change right away. You will see them smile, and they may even give you a compliment in return. It will make them feel better and you will feel better too.

Giving compliments may not be easy for you at first. You may have to start by practicing on your family or your best friend. If you will try it, it will become easier and the more you do it, the more you will see just how powerful a few kind words can be.

2. Say "Thank you."

It's amazing that when children are young parents say that all the time. They constantly remind their kids, "Say, 'Thank you.'" Somehow, though, when kids hit 10 or 12, it seems those words go completely out of their vocabulary. We seem to forget that there are a lot of people who spend a lot of time and money and worry just for us. Saying "thank you" doesn't cost us anything. It doesn't take hardly any time at all and, yet, it is an amazing way to give back to someone who has served you.

Saying "thank you" has an almost magical power. I don't know exactly how it works, but I've seen it happen. Try it and you'll be amazed to find that as you remember to say "thank you," you will find that more will come your way and you'll have much more to be thankful for. Try it.

3. Serve someone with your words.

You would be amazed to see the results of what can happen if you will forget yourself and serve someone else with your words.

What I mean is, think about how many people there are who could really use a kind words and a conversation. There are thousands of people in rest homes. There are children in homeless shelters. There are your own grandparents, a person you know who lives alone, a friend who is in the hospital or someone who has recently moved to your area. You would be performing a tremendous service by forgetting about yourself for just a few minutes and by sharing a conversation, by asking them about themselves or by letting them know you care.

4. Learn a new word.

When I was in middle school and my friends were cussing all the time, I thought, "Man, is that the only word you know?" Since then, I have realized how fun it is to learn new words—and to try words with more than four letters!

If you hear your mom or dad or a teacher or other adult use a word you don't know, ask them what it means. If you hear a new word at school, look it up in a dictionary and then try using it yourself. Write down new words you hear and try to use them in a sentence. Make it a game and you'll find it can be a lot of fun.

You'll find as you increase your vocabulary you will be able to express yourself better and find new ways to describe things—without having to use the same (four-letter!) word in every sentence.

5. Have fun with words.

Have fun with words by playing a game. Do a crossword puzzle. Play a word-search game. Or, make a word picture. Pick a word like "Happy," or "Joy," "Brave" or "Smile" or whatever word you want to focus on or a word that is important to you. Then make a colorful poster or drawing with that word in the center. Put it up on your wall or mirror as a reminder to make that word a part of your day. Smile!

6. Memorize a poem, a quote or a passage of scripture.

There are hundreds and hundreds of positive poems, religious passages or helpful quotes that can remind you about what is most important to you. It is a fun exercise to try to memorize one of these poems or a part of a story. By memorizing something that is uplifting and positive, you can go back to that at any time, no matter what is going on around you.

7. Explore some great examples of language.

You can explore a whole new world of ideas and interesting language. It may seem like a big stretch to go to a Shakespeare play or to read an essay by Socrates. But, if you look at it like an adventure, like cool investigation or a puzzle to figure out, you will learn some awesome things. Here are some things you could explore:

+ Ask your parents to take you to a play or read a play in a book. One good one you may want to check out is by George Bernhard Shaw. It's called "Pygmalion" and it was later made into the movie called, "My Fair Lady." In it, a flower girl who basically lived on the streets was completely changed when she learned how to speak proper English. Her station in life improved. Other people looked at her differently and her self-confidence improved.

+ For a fun and challenging exploration of cool language, check out the Declaration of Independence or the Constitution of the United States of America.

+ Read some of the greatest speeches of all time. See if you can discover who said, "Give me liberty or give me death"; or, "Four score and seven years ago…"; or, "I have a dream"; or, "Ask not what your country can do for you…"

+ Try getting into some of the great books, like books known as the classics. Even stories they call "children's stories," like "Cinderella" and "Beauty and the Beast," are fun to read as full-length books. Ask your librarian for a suggestion!

Keep a Language that Lifts Journal

All of these suggestions about using language that lifts are important, but this one is really cool because you can use a Language that Lifts journal to bring everything together and to keep track of how you're doing.

We've created a sample page to get you started. The idea is to keep track of the ways you use language to lift others.

My Language that Lifts Journal

Date:

Today I Said: **To:**

Thank you

Please

You are really awesome at

_____

I really appreciate you doing

_____

Can I help you?

Other Cool Ways I Used Language that Lifts Today:

My Thoughts and Feelings About Today:

"Leave People Better Than You Found Them"

Just like a baseball player keeps stats in order to improve, this journal can help you see your progress and, also, can show you things you maybe need to work harder on.

You will see that, at the top of the journal page are some positive words and phrases. These are words that you can practice using every day to help lift someone else and make their day a little better. You can make copies of the journal pages and keep them in your school notebook. That way, during the day, you can check off the times you used one of these positive words and phrases. Or, keep your Language that Lifts journal at home and then, once a day, like, after school or just before you go to bed, check off the positive things you did that day.

Then, write some of your own feelings on the lines at the bottom of the journal page. Write down the things you think about and the ways you are trying to improve. You may even want to keep track of how other people respond to you when you use language that lifts. This journal can be a great way for you to see how words are making a difference in your life. After a few months, you will be able to look back through your journal and see the effects you've had on people as well as yourself.

Have a Language that Lifts assembly or workshop

All the suggestions I've already shared are things you can do to improve on your own. A lot of people say it helps to have their whole school or church group or neighborhood involved in making language better. On our Web site (www.NoCussing.com) you can learn about the "Language that Lifts" peer-to-peer school assembly presentation. I would love to visit your school or community group, so, please check it out!

I hope these few suggestions will help and that you will soon be finding all kinds of ways to lift yourself and others with the language that you use. I look forward to hearing how you do as you use language to

"Leave People Better Than You Found Them."

15
Start Your Own
No Cussing Club Chapter

A lot of people have asked how they can start a No Cussing Club chapter in their area, and if you are one of those, congratulations! Starting a No Cussing Club chapter is a great way of leaving people better than you found them. It's also a great way to keep yourself cuss free—because now you have a whole chapter watching you and helping you keep the No Cussing Challenge.

Before I get into how to start a chapter, let me say something else. I have heard about some great things that have been done in schools to help students improve the way they talk and the way they act.

In Salina, Kansas, at Salina Central High School, where they have about 1,000 students, they had a whole program of improving their school and of supporting positive behavior among the students. What they did was send students into the classrooms to talk to their peers about what they wanted to see improved and changed in their schools. Basically, they asked the question, "What do we need to do to make this a better place to be?" They had student leaders from all different groups at the school who went into each of the English classes to ask this question. What the student leaders found out was that one of the "hot topics" that students mentioned over and over was: "We don't like the profanity at the school."

One of the art teachers and some of the students were chosen to work on that particular "hot topic." They started "Cussbusters" and put up Cussbuster posters, did things on the announcements, made buttons for kids to wear and taught the students about cussing and how to stop. Shelda Burger, the counselor at Salina Central, says, "That was three years ago. The posters are still here and the profanity has lessened tremendously."

I love hearing stories like this and hearing how we really can work together to encourage better language. It's great to see things like this out there. So, if you already have a program or have tried to stop cussing, that's great! We would still welcome you in the No Cussing Club and you will find it won't conflict but would maybe add to anything else you might be doing. What that means is that the No Cussing Club is also a great thing for Scout troops, sports teams, church groups or others that have a lot of other good things going on as well. Taking the No Cussing Club Challenge or starting a No Cussing Club chapter will only make what you are already doing even better.

Let me tell you about a kid named Dallin Huso, who started a No Cussing Club chapter in Arizona. Dallin is a cool kid who likes sports like basketball, soccer and football. His other hobbies are reading, writing books, and playing instruments.

He says, like me, he saw a lot of his friends start cussing in fifth and sixth grade, but Dallin didn't think that was the right thing to do.

"My parents have told me that people show respect through language, and that language tells a lot about a person," Dallin said. "I think that words have a lot of meaning and that words do tell a lot about a person."

Dallin said something else that I have thought about a lot too. "The purpose of the No Cussing Club is to help kids not to cuss, and also, if they can say no to cussing, then it will be easier to say no to drugs and all of the other bad things in the world."

Isn't that a cool thing to think about—how saying no to something small like cussing could help you say no to the bigger things too.

"Some kids thought it was cool that I was doing this, but others thought I was stupid for doing it," Dallin says. But, he didn't let that stop him and he now has about 40 members in his chapter. He says the chapter members wear their orange No Cussing Club T-shirts to school every Friday.

"At club meetings, we give out the T-shirts and certificates to members who have just joined. We also recite the No Cussing Challenge. We ask kids if they have had some experiences with the No Cussing Club that they would like to share, and we talk about substitutes for cuss words and things like that."

Some kids have asked Dallin, "Why should we join, if we don't cuss?"

He tells them that by joining the No Cussing Club they can encourage other kids to not cuss.

"Maybe kids who do cuss will see that you're a cool person, and that you don't cuss, so then that person might stop cussing too," Dallin tells them.

Rachael Eyington started a No Cussing Club chapter in Las Vegas, Nevada, and their chapter is now an official club at her school, Harney Middle School.

She said, at her school, "There is an unbelievable amount of kids that cuss in every sentence that they say."

She says it bothers her to hear the cussing and the insults and "when people purposely say something about someone behind their backs."

Rachel likes to play soccer and she also likes to draw, sing and play piano. She thinks the No Cussing Club can help "to make the world a better place and help kids and adults around Las Vegas, one step at a time."

While working on cleaning up their language, the chapter also plans to help clean up their city, with "activities that help the environment and things that help Las Vegas be a cleaner and better place."

So, check it out. Here is a checklist of all kinds of good reasons to start a No Cussing Club chapter in your area. See which things sound like you:

Good Reasons to Start a No Cussing Club Chapter

Put a check by each one of these statements that you agree with. If you check two or more, you may want to consider starting a No Cussing Club chapter.

- ❏ Cussing bothers me and I would like to hang out with people who don't cuss.
- ❏ I want to help other kids see how they can stop cussing.
- ❏ I want some help and support so I don't start cussing.
- ❏ I like the idea of starting a club that is fun and that encourages kids to use language that lifts.
- ❏ I think a No Cussing Club chapter would make my school or neighborhood a better place.
- ❏ I like ORANGE...so I want to see everyone wearing a No Cussing Club T-shirt!

So, you wanna start an NCC chapter in your area?
Cool! Here's how you do it …

Step 1—Become a Member—it's FREE!

To sign up as a member of the No Cussing Club, all you need to do is to go to www.NoCussing.com and click on the "Become a member" tab. Fill in your information and you will have access to the "Members Only" page. There you can get your free certificate and other cool stuff.

Step 2—Get Your Friends to Join.

Make a flyer and pass it around to friends at school, family, and church friends. You can go to our Web site and download the flyer that we used when we had our first meeting. Remember, sometimes just deciding to do it is the hard part. When we did it, we had a lot of interest from a lot of kids and we had no problem getting kids to join. Some of their parents and other adults wanted to join too.

Step 3—Get a Sponsor.

- What is a sponsor? A sponsor is someone who will help pay for your club's activities. While you don't have to have a sponsor, you will find that having a sponsor—even if it's your mom or dad—will help you keep things going.
- What will they pay for? Your club T-shirts.
- Why will they do it? A sponsor will agree to help you because they like your cause and it will be good advertisement for their company or organization to be involved with a club that is helping kids be better. Let them know your club will wear the T-shirts every Friday and that the shirts will have their company's name on them.

There are many companies, organizations or even individuals who would be more than happy to sponsor your No Cussing Club. Go to a local business or someone you know who has a business. Ask if they will sponsor your club. Tell them you will be passing out 50 T-shirts with their name on it as the sponsor. You can order these customized T-shirts, with printing on the front and back, from our Web site and the cost is minimal. Check our Web site for current prices. We keep them as low as possible so you can let sponsors know they will be getting a great deal for the advertisement they will get when your 50 chapter members will be wearing the shirts every week. Most businesses have a budget that will cover advertisement or sponsorships.

A real estate company was our first sponsor and they paid for all of our shirts. And they also signed up for the No Cussing Club!

Step 4—Have your First No Cussing Club Meeting.

Have a meeting at your house. You may want to have pizza or refreshments. Your sponsor may agree to pay for refreshments for the first meeting or you could have some of your friends bring a bag of cookies each or something. Keep it simple. Make it fun. Give everyone a T-shirt and a copy of the No Cussing Club certificate.

You may want to nominate a chapter president, vice president and secretary. You can divide up responsibilities which may include:

+ Getting new members.
+ Organizing meetings. (We suggest holding a meeting once a month or every other month.)
+ Reminding members to wear their T-shirts on Fridays.

♦ Planning activities—The motto of the No Cussing Club is "Leave People Better Than You Found Them." As a chapter, you may want to do activities that support that motto. Clean up your local park, do graffiti removal, visit a retirement home, or anything like that. (At some schools, activities like this will count toward community service requirements.) Visit your local city government and ask them for ways your club can help the community.

Remember, one of the great things about having your own chapter is that you will be able to do even more to "Leave People Better Than You Found Them!"

Step 5—Register your NCC Chapter.

We want to know you're out there! Register your No Cussing Club chapter on our Web site. Feel free to let us know if you would like some help getting your No Cussing Club chapter started!

Step 6—Be in the News!

Call your local news station and local paper and let them know about your club. You can also download the Sample Media Release from our Web site and then change it to include your name and city, and your own comments. Then, fax or e-mail it to your local newspaper, radio station and TV station. You may be surprised, our local paper was very happy to cover our story and they like to receive any updates about what we are doing on a local or national level. Be sure to mention your sponsor in your media release.

One more word about starting a No Cussing Club

Now, one more thing about starting a No Cussing Club chapter. Some people may think that your language has to be perfect all the time if you are going to start a chapter. But, that isn't true. If, when you start, you still cuss once in while, that's not a big deal. The whole idea of having a No Cussing Club is not to punish people or kick them out if they haven't quite gotten out of the habit of cussing. The club offers support and reminds members of their goals. So, this girl from Australia has the right idea:

You've Got Mail

Dear McKay,

I cuss a lot and can't stop but when I was sitting and watching Dr. Phil, and you came on, it really changed the way I think. You know what? You are a real hero and I am going to try and start my own No Cussing Club.... Just watch, in like a million years you will still be remembered for all the hard work you have done.

The thing is, all of my friends are always swearing and then after hearing them, I kind of get in the same habit, but with what you said, you have changed me a lot and you are my hero.

—Name withheld

Destiny

There you have it. I went from being dumpster bait at my own high school to having an e-mail like the one I just shared, with someone all the way in Australia saying, "You are my hero." But don't worry, I'm not asking for trophies or anything like that. The real point in even sharing that is to tell you this—the only reason someone has called me a hero, the only reason I've been on national television, the only reason I could even write this book is because of you. That's right, every single person who has joined the No Cussing Club or even thought about joining has helped to make it what it is today. At first, yeah, it was about me and my little group of friends at my middle school. But all that changed as each person came on board and started to make the No Cussing Club their own. Now it sort of has a life of its own.

YOU are the real hero

People are joining the club and chapters are being started all over, so the number of members keeps growing—but the really amazing thing isn't in all the thousands of people who are joining. The real story is that the No Cussing Club is affecting people's lives—one kid, or one adult at a time. These people are really the heroes—you are a hero—because you are the ones who are making a choice to stand up and make a difference. You are the ones who may have been bullied, you are the ones who may have felt like you were the only one standing up for what was right, yet you have done it—hundreds, thousands of you have done it! That's what has made this club so strong: It's the strength of people like you.

And I owe you a big thank you for it! Have you got any idea how different my life is now? It was a strange feeling to go back to school after summer vacation my sophomore year. I remembered well those first few weeks of being a freshman. I remembered Club Rush and the horrors of what I went through with kids cussing me out and getting in my face. I remember feeling like my No Cussing Club T-shirt was like a glowing, neon orange sign, pointing the way for all the bullies to find me and make fun of me.

I remember having question after question thrown at me—

- "What makes cussing so bad?"
- "Who do you think you are, the cussing police?"
- "Why don't you mind your own business?"
- "Why are you trying to take away my First Amendment right?"
- "What makes you think you know so much?"

That's just the point. I didn't know so much. But it has been those questions and the many questions from television and news reporters that have helped me figure it all out and to learn some important things about language and, especially, about people.

It's almost like some of the bad stuff has helped me be better. It was the questions and accusations that helped make me stronger, it was the bad days of bullying and all the cyberbullying that helped me see just how that feels, and made me want to be kinder to others too.

So far, I haven't seen the inside of a trash can and a lot of the teasing has calmed down. When I'm at school, I don't feel alone anymore. I see people I know and a lot of kids say hi to me and talk to me in the halls. Every once in awhile, some dude cusses me out. But now, even kids who aren't members of the No Cussing Club stick up for me. It's kind of cool.

The No Cussing Club—Alive and Thriving

Many of the clubs that were there on that first Club Rush day aren't around anymore. I remember being told, many times, back when we had less than 100 members, that our club wouldn't last a month. But here we are. The No Cussing Club is still very much here. It's alive and it's growing. We are still getting members everyday—all because of people like you.

I know for many of you it hasn't been easy to take the No Cussing Challenge and you may still be thinking, "How could I ever stand up to others around me? It's, like, everyone talks that way."

A story I just heard from a church group youth leader reminded me of how true that is for most young people today. I know this is the kind of environment you live in every day.

The youth group leader's story reminded me all over again that, even though things may seem better for me, others still have to deal with this every day. Here's what he said:

"Last week, I was teaching a lesson to a church youth group. There were 15 young men ranging from 7th graders to high school seniors. The lesson moved into a discussion of language and its effects on us individually and as a society.

"This group was a typical representation of young men from our community. In this group, we had the shy wall flowers as well as the class clowns, the jocks as well as the 'gamers' (who call themselves nerds), the studious as well as those who are barely making the grade.

"I brought up the subject of profanity, and there were the expected giggles, whisperings and smirks, but instead of just ignoring it and throwing out my opinion of what they 'should' do, I really wanted to know what these kids faced on a daily basis. So I asked the boys what they felt the situation was like at their schools with regards to profanity. The room erupted with conversation, several boys trying to speak to me at once, private conversations in the back of the room, and conversations across the room. The feeling was unanimous. They said profanity was everywhere at their schools—elementary, middle and high school.

"One of the high school seniors said that as he and his friend walked to school one morning, he said, 'Let's try an experiment and see how long it takes until we hear the 'F' word.' He said that it took about 20 seconds.

"Another boy said that some kids at school use the 'F' word in every sentence. Normally, I might have taken this as an exaggeration. But I had an experience of my own a few months earlier that corroborated his statement. One day, as I drove my son home from the local middle school, my attention was drawn to a group of three high school boys walking home. Because the high school, middle school and elementary school are all within close proximity to each other, everyday, at around 2:30 to 3:00 in the afternoon, the streets are filled with kids of all ages walking home. There was nothing about their appearance that drew my attention to these three boys. They were just three modest-looking boys from one of our local, middle income neighborhoods. But, what drew my attention was their language. Our car windows were rolled down as we passed by. I could not discern the subject or context of their discussion. But I could not mistake the 'F' word uttered at least five times in five sentences. There was no shock or feeling discomfort apparent in his companions. Neither was there laughter. There simply was no reaction at all. There was nothing to suggest that this type of conversation was out of the norm for these kids. Additionally, they did not seem to sense any requirement for discretion or to keep their foul language from being heard by the younger children around them. At that time, I had no idea of the onslaught the boys in my church's youth group faced each day."

It WILL get better

I know for many, many of you taking the No Cussing Challenge may be a scary thing. I promise you that it **will** get better and you will find a lot of support when you do take a stand. My hope is that the No Cussing Club will continue to go on so that anybody, anywhere can have that support to help them in some small way to do what may seem hard at first but that will make a big and very positive difference.

My hope is that the members of this club—that you and others around the world—will think about what cussing really is—all the things we talked about at the beginning of the book and that you will help put a stop to the swearing, the profanity and the "F" words as well as the "trash talk" and the horrible things that are said about individual cultures or religions.

I've had some people laugh about that and say to me, "Why don't you go help someone who is starving or do something else that is really important?" But, from all the stories I get, from all the people who say not cussing was a first step to making better choices in every part of their life, I have seen that this **is** really important—much more important than some people imagine.

Two parts to the Challenge

So, I do hope you will remember the "Don't Cuss" part of the Challenge, but I also want to remind you that there are two parts to the No Cussing Club Challenge.

The first part, the No Cussing Challenge is more of an inward challenge. It's a commitment you make to yourself. You promise not to cuss and to use more positive language. Those positive words then affect your thoughts and your view of the world.

The second part, the "Leave People Better Than You Found Them" part, is an outward challenge. It's a commitment you make to help others. You clean up your language and keep it positive and your positive words and actions affect people around you.

So, really, taking the No Cussing Challenge means that you are going to go out and make an effort everyday to make a difference in somebody else's life. It could be something big, but it doesn't always have to be. It might be small, quiet, and unnoticeable to others. Maybe just a smile to someone you see who really needs it. Maybe it's a kind word to someone who's feeling down. Maybe it's reaching out in friendship to someone who looks lonely.

One of my cousins is a great example of this. My cousin noticed that there was a girl at her school who sat by herself all the time. Nobody would talk to her. The girl was very over-weight and her hair was always messy and hung down in her face. My cousin noticed how lonely she looked. So, one day at lunch, my cousin decided to go over and talk to her. She told her friends that she wanted to bring the girl over to the lunch table where they were all sitting, but they said, "No way." They even told my cousin to stay away from the girl because they said she was weird. My cousin talked to the girl, then continued to go over during lunch and talk with her every day after that. She noticed that the girl started to smile and talk more. Then, one day, my cousin invited her to her house. They put makeup on together and my cousin curled her hair. The girl also invited my cousin over to her house. My cousin said it was very dark and cluttered in the house. She said it was very quiet and felt cold and sad.

Eventually, other kids joined them and started hanging out with my cousin and the girl during lunch. Soon the girl had many of her own friends. What if my cousin had never followed that feeling to talk with her that day? It's amazing how one person can make such a big difference in someone's life by doing something that seems so small at first.

There are kids at every school who are bullied, picked on or left out. Sometimes we may not even be aware that these things are happening. It's not always easy to see the sadness or loneliness inside of others. But, we all have had times when we are down and we know what's it's like to feel left out sometimes. We really don't have to look far to find someone who could use a smile or a friendly word. Just doing some small, kind thing can make a real difference.

These last two e-mails sum it up pretty well and they show how you, too, can make a difference by doing small, simple things:

You've Got Mail

Dear McKay,

I work at a local college in the dining hall where profanity runs rampant. On one occasion, a fellow employee was designing a Christmas scene on the windows for the holiday season. Sitting nearby were college students cussing profusely. I asked them to refrain from using profanity and be considerate of the young lady who was painting and could not move until her work was done. They said if she was bothered by it, she would have spoken up herself. Well, I know this woman and she is meek and mild-mannered and would not have spoken to them. This incident made me realize that people using bad language were not always aware that it offended other people.

I decided to make my own handmade badge with the sign *"No Profanity"* and began wearing it. It was my way of taking a stand on this issue. I myself do not cuss and prefer eating in an environment that is not polluted with profanity. I am also concerned because the dining room is open to the public and we have prospective students and their parents visiting our school on a daily basis. I personally do not think it is good business to have a bunch of foul-mouthed college students spewing cuss words into the atmosphere. The ironic thing is that I was approached by a fellow employee who asked me who the "No Profanity" sign was for since he said the staff was just as guilty of swearing!

When I go back to school after break, I will be sporting the new No Cussing badge! Thanks for standing up for what you believe in, and taking it one step further so the world can help become a better place and we can "leave people better than we found them."

    —Linda Studer

       ◆ ◆ ◆

Dear McKay,

When I heard about your No Cussing Club, I said to myself, "That's a brave young man. He's going to get

a lot of flak for his stance. I wonder how he'll hold up?"
I heard through the grapevine that you've been teased
and taunted and even threatened, but that you have
stayed your course. You have stuck with who you are
in the face of adversity. I have cussed almost all my
life, especially when my computer hasn't worked right.
I taught my kids to cuss. Of course, they had plenty of
help from others. I'm cutting down on my cussing, and
I hope my kids follow my lead.

Your courage has given me pause and challenged
me to be a better man in another way, too. Last year,
I was dealing with some unpleasant side effects from
a serious medical operation, and I got into the habit
of drinking alcohol at night to escape. I wasn't proud
of it, but I kept doing it. Then I thought about you and
your refusal to let pain and ridicule dissuade you from
your high course. I realized I wasn't being the best I
could be. For one thing, if there had been a family
emergency, I couldn't have driven a car safely. And,
of course, I knew that running away doesn't solve anything. I thought, "If McKay Hatch can be tough enough
to proceed with gusto even when it's hard, so can I."
And, I did. I chose to face my challenges straight on,
sober, with my head held high.

So you see, what you are doing with your No Cussing
Club has consequences beyond what you initially envi-
sioned. It inspires us all to do what's right, even when
no one is looking. So, I say thanks, and keep up the
good work. I aspire to be as honorable and bold as you.

  —Name withheld

If each of us can leave someone better than we found them,
if each of us can have an effect on just one person, then it can
become a chain reaction.

That is what our second No Cussing Club song is all about.
The song is called "Waves" and it is about being the one to start
that chain reaction.

Waves

It's like a stone upon the shore
That is cast into the sea
And the ripples that it makes
Become waves
Crashing down
On you and me

It's the things you do and say
That you cast into this world
From soul to soul they go
Making waves
Crashing down
On you and me

I'm sending out a new vibration
To touch one soul or move a nation

Gonna send it out
Gonna send it out
Yeah

It's such a simple little thing
That confounds the wisest men
And you're where it begins
Make waves
And crash'em down
On you and me

So send it out your new vibration
To touch one soul or move a nation

Gotta send it out
Ya gotta send it out
Yeah

It's the things you do and say
That you cast into this world
From soul to soul they grow
To waves
Crashing down
On you and me

Words do have meaning! The words you say to others, the words you think to yourself, do have a powerful impact.

Words can affect the way you feel and the way you see the world. When I give talks at schools and to other groups of kids, I use a quote that has come to mean more and more to me as I understand it more. I tell them: "Your words become your thoughts, your thoughts become your actions, your actions become your character, and your character becomes your destiny."

The more I think about this statement, the more I believe it.

So, like I told my friends, "Don't Cuss!" Go to www.No Cussing.com and take the Challenge today that will lift you and others.

Think positive words, use positive words, and leave people better than you found them. If you do this, I know you will have a positive future. It's your destiny!

McKay Hatch

No Cussing Club Founder

No Cussing Club wristbands, T-shirts
or other No Cussing Club items,
as well as additional copies of this book
are available for purchase at:
www.NoCussing.com

♦ ♦ ♦

"Language that Lifts" Presentations

McKay Hatch is available for
school presentations or youth functions.
To learn more about his "Language that Lifts" presentations
and how to schedule him for your school or youth group,
go to **www.NoCussing.com.**

Educators from across the nation highly recommend
McKay's presentation!

For parents, teachers and leaders:

Many schools and youth groups who have had
McKay speak during the day also have provided
an evening workshop for parents, teachers and leaders
presented by
McKay's parents, Brent and Phelecia Hatch,
authors of *Raising a G-Rated Family in an X-Rated World.*
More information about their presentation is available on
www.BrentHatch.com.